OF THE HOUSE OF JOB

By LG Bond

Trilogy Christian Publishers

A Wholly Owned Subsidiary of Trinity Broadcasting Network

2442 Michelle Drive

Tustin, CA 92780

For information, address Trilogy Christian Publishing

Rights Department, 2442 Michelle Drive, Tustin, Ca 92780.

Trilogy Christian Publishing/ TBN and colophon are trademarks of Trinity Broadcasting Network.

For information about special discounts for bulk purchases, please contact Trilogy Christian Publishing.

Manufactured in the United States of America

10 9 8 7 6 5 4 3 2 1

Library of Congress Cataloging-in-Publication Data is available.

ISBN 978-1-64773-943-0

ISBN 978-1-64773-944-7 (ebook)

DEDICATION

To my beloved blessings,

Lela "Bug," Cynthia "Cynner," and Bear Joyner;

God used my relationship with you to help me identify and connect with Job's wife and what she might have been feeling or thinking while enduring her fate as Job's wife.

ACKNOWLEDGMENTS

My God: To You alone be the glory and honor in any and all good things I do! Thank You, Father!

My Sweet Husband: You have boldly taken this leap of faith with me. Thank you, Jeffery, for supporting me!

My Family: God has used you in many ways to shape who I am and how I think. Thank you!

My Ladies: There are many of you who have supported, encouraged, and guided me over the years. But these have helped me on this journey:

> Edith Breland — I was living with her when this story first came to be.

> Martha Clark — She encouraged me to share what God had laid on my heart.

> Dr. Betty Hassler — My first editor.

Without you, Ladies, this book would not even exist. Thank you all!

DISCLAIMER

This is a fictional dramatization of Job's life based on the book of Job in the Bible using various translations (NIV, KJV, NAS, etc.) that helped in the telling of this story. Although the plot and some content have been taken from the biblical account, this story should not be read as literally true. I, the author, have chosen a modern era since the Bible does not give a clear timeline for this story.

The concept for this perspective was born from these questions:

1. What would cause a godly woman to ever say to anyone, "Curse God"[1]?
   Answer: Maybe she was not a godly woman.

2. What would cause any woman who was married to such a godly man[2] to ever say, "Curse God and die!" to him?
   Answer: I give you "Of the House of Job."

…along with my personal experience of being separated from my beloved children due to circumstances out of my control, although admittedly, some of my mistakes had fostered such circumstances.

Further, I suggest and encourage: read the Biblical account of Job's story either before or after reading this.

---

1 Job 2:9, NIV
2 Job 1:1, KJV

PRELUDE

Jah was a happy woman. She had a good husband by anyone's standards. Job was one of the wealthiest men in the land. He owned livestock, land, along with many men and women he employed. Some were with them just to pay off a debt that Job had covered for them. In fact, most started that way. However, there were a few who chose to serve Job for life; they were like family.

The family wanted for nothing. To her, Job was perfect: God-fearing, wise, strong, and patient. He didn't talk down to her like most other men spoke to women. He valued her opinion, recognized her intellect, and appreciated her as his wife and the manager of the household.

She, too, had no cause to complain. She had given birth to seven sturdy sons and three beautiful daughters, who even now, though they were out on their own, and to her delight, still enjoyed each other's company. They regularly cycled through each of the sons' homes, enjoying life and a daily family feast. These feast days[3] proceeded in the order of their birth, beginning at Erel's home, then to Tavis' house, on to Tamas's, Cobus's, Yakov's, Jaakko's, and lastly to Giacobbe's. After their time of feasting, the siblings returned home, and the cycle started over again. Her girls — Rada, Xenia, and Abby — were invited, along with their brothers.

Her husband Job would rise early every morning to make a sacrifice for that day's feast on behalf of them all.

---

3 Job 1:4-5, NAS

It was something her husband insisted upon. "What if one day Jaakko says something cleverer than Erel, but Erel wins in a contest of strength? And in their 'friendly' jeering, Jaakko curses God in his heart for his brother's strength, or Erel does the same for his brother's cleverness?" Job feared God's anger towards them and wanted protection for them all.

No, Jah had no reason in the world to ever want anything but the life she enjoyed.

That was before…before that day. The day she wished never happened, and the day none would ever forget. The pain of that day was a deep, gouging scar on her heart for the rest of her life.

FOREWARD

The Old Testament Book of Job is one of the most familiar stories in the Bible. Job's life has all the elements of a best-selling novel: wealth and prosperity, tragic losses, loneliness and despair, and—of course—a happy ending. Perhaps this last element has robbed present day readers of feeling the magnitude of Job's suffering and his heart-wrenching struggle to maintain his faith.

Sensing God's leadership to undertake a re-telling of Job's story, Loretta Bond brings to life images and characters that perhaps have grown stale to many who've read the Bible account many times. She gives these people names and identifying characteristics. She has the courage to include beloved slaves in Job's household. Since many Bible scholars place these events in the time of the Patriarchs, Job may have lived during the days of Abraham. And we know Abraham owned slaves (Gen. 17:27).

We know Job was not a nomad. He owned houses and lands. We know he lived in community. He had friends who heard of his plight. And we know he had a family that he dearly loved. Because we know little about the dwellings and everyday household customs of these early God-fearing people, Loretta puts the characters in familiar surroundings similar to other biblical stories. From her tender heart, Loretta weaves these elements into a fictionalized tale based on Scriptural truth: if you have reason to doubt God's love or His sovereignty, look to Job. The purpose in her writing is to show that, despite outward circumstances, faith leads us to encounter an omniscient and omnipotent God. Although Job has many questions, he finds that knowing Him is answer enough.

When I first got to know Loretta, we discovered a mutual love for discipling believers. Through writing fictional accounts, we also discovered that discipleship can be nurtured through storytelling. Perhaps that's why Jesus is known as the world's greatest storyteller. We are humbled to follow in His steps.

Betty J Hassler, Ph.D.
Author, Trophies of Grace:
Four Novellas in One Volume
Pace, Florida, December 2020

CONTENTS

CHAPTER 1

The day started in a typical manner. Jah awoke early, just as the light hit the ornate stained glass of the small round window, the only one in the room. This window was a special gift from her husband. He had hued the pane opening by hand with the help of their sons when they were still living under one roof. One of the hired hands, who was working off a large debt Job had agreed to cover, was skilled at tempering and staining glass. The whole clan had enjoyed watching the progression. The man expedited the repayment of his debt in the process.

When she was sure her husband was also awake, she kissed him gently. Then she retreated outdoors to oversee the preparation of his breakfast before a full day's work.

That night, her children were going to be feasting at Erel's, which was the farthest away from the main house and was a new stone building. She desired to send them some of her famous fig bread that they loved so much. Of course, she and Job had an open invitation to the feasts, but they felt the youngsters needed not to be burdened with them. With all the work they tended to daily, they hadn't the energy to stay up any later than usual. The older they became, the longer the work seemed to take, and the shorter the days seemed to get.

Jah joined the couple they would eat with, who were among their oldest and dearest employees. They had already begun the usual tasks for the start of any day. Jah felt God had sent Keziah to her personally.

Keziah could run Jah's household without her if she had to, a fact Keziah had proven while she was pregnant with her only child. Jah had come down with the most unusual fever. They had tried everything they knew to break it. And yet it was two full days before anyone, other than the four of them around the fire now, had any inclination that something was amiss.

Yes, Jah was grateful for Keziah, as was Job for her mate, Kadri. The couple was younger than them, but at their meals together, they were treated as equals, free to share their opinions, within the bounds of their culture. Respect for the master and mistress of the household was held in very high esteem.

Job came outside and sat on logs near the open fire to oversee that everything was handled properly. When the light yet hearty breakfast of the bread from the day before, fresh ewe's milk, newly harvested fruit, nuts and seeds was finished, the men ventured out to their tasks of preparing the day's sacrifice, while the women cleared away the remnants and continued with their daily chores. They would reconvene at midday, if possible, to discuss what new tasks needed to be addressed, and then again in the evening for a recap of the day's events before retiring for the night.

Each day expected specific tasks to be done, and everyone knew their customary responsibilities. Everyone was routinely expected to be able to at least lend a helping hand in any chore. To cut the monotony and ensure that if someone fell ill, the work would still be tended to, a rotation was commonly practiced.

That day, Jah went about her morning joyfully humming a tune under her breath. She looked forward to the possibility of seeing her husband at lunch. She started on her fig bread first thing so it would be ready to send to Erel's house in time for their feast. She made enough for Job and Kadri to have some at their lunch if the dough rose in time. A few other loaves would be passed around for everyone else in the camp.

Keren, a new house girl, observed Jah and Keziah with such wonderment that she could not contain her thoughts, "You two move as one spirit!"

"Child!" Keziah scolded Keren for her unprompted comment.

"Keziah, it's okay. What do you mean?" Jah wondered. She leaned her back against the stone walls of the house. She was facing the girl, who was sitting at a low wooden table in the corner.

Embarrassed, Keren replied, "Forgive my outburst, my lady…" Jah nodded her acceptance and motioned her to continue, "…but you and Keziah move together like in a dance." The girl rose and twirled about the room. "Almost as one…never getting in each other's way." At that, she almost ran into Keziah, who was standing like a mighty unmovable tree with her arms crossed. Moving away from Keziah's fearsome stare, Keren stammered, "I've never seen two people so in-tune with one another." She sat back on her stool and continued the sewing and mending she had been given for the day.

Jah just smiled at the child's observation. She and Keziah had many years of experience being with each other, enough to anticipate one another. They shared a mutual glance, then Keziah motioned the youngster to get back to work and not bother herself with what she or the mistress were doing. Later, the girl prepared the midday meal and, after delivering loaves to everyone, was released to join her own blood kin in their quarters.

The bread was piping hot; its smell filled the air. Job and Kadri arrived, led by their appetites, and having broad grins. "What did we ever do to be blessed with fig bread?" Job asked Kadri over his shoulder as they entered to sit for the rejuvenating spread.

Kadri eagerly replied, "I'm not sure, but whatever it is, I hope we do it again and often." He swung his right leg over the stool where Keren had been sewing and took his place.

The women said nothing but smiled appreciatively. They sat to join them.

Job prayed, "Thank you, Lord, for the blessing of this bounty and the hands that have prepared it."

Jah opened the conversation, "Are the oxen plowing the north field?"

"Yes, with the donkeys grazing nearby. Gilad is overseeing them," Job answered.

"We can send him the leftover bread from our meal," Keziah suggested.

"Yes, and whoever takes it to him can take the loaf to Erel's house as well," Jah agreed.

"I'll go," Kadri offered, "I need to check on the well we dug last week for the camels. Eitan said they had seen bandits in the area."

"Just be careful. You take whomever you need with you," Job instructed.

"Will do so."

Keziah spoke up, "Good. You can also take Abby the blanket I made her."

"How is Cale taking to being a shepherd?" Jah asked. Cale was the couple's only son. The baby of their litter, Abby, was very taken with him and he with her.

"He says it is peaceful...Can you believe it? Sheep? Peaceful?" Kadri wondered.

"He is your son!" Keziah teased.

"He is a fine boy, just fine," Job beamed, "I'll send a relief for him so he can join us tonight for an update."

"Wonderful idea!" Jah exclaimed.

The younger couple was pleased by the prospect of being reunited with their son that very evening. They finished their meal, and each returned to their duties. Jah's extensive cantonment buzzed with activity. Meanwhile, others went to the four corners of the vast estate to tend to the tasks that had been assigned during the meal.

By the evening meal, the only ones left about the main house were the three women. Soon, Job arrived, but Kadri and Cale were late. Job wondered what was keeping them. He left to wait for them outside, to not unduly alarm the womenfolk.

Keren had been recruited to serve the evening meal. She was excited. Rumor had it that the master treated Kadri, Keziah, and their son Cale as members of his family instead of just hired hands. Perhaps one day, she would also be in this coveted position.

Keziah took her aside, "Keren, you have been chosen to serve at the meal tonight because we — that is the master — trust that you are loyal. Loyal enough to keep whatever confidences are discussed, implied, or shown in your presence tonight. Kadri and I wouldn't have our position in this household for this long if we had loose lips. Just the opposite, in fact."

Keziah tried to express that this was possibly the child's opportunity to be set apart from the others, to be chosen by the master for privileged work. She would have never admitted out loud that she and her mistress needed a reliable, stronger, younger body to make the work easier for them. Keziah unconsciously massaged her aching hip joint. However, she also wanted the girl to understand and not let the honor go to her head, "The master and his wife are very noble and deserve all respect. Do you understand?"

"I believe so...Yes! Whatever happens tonight at dinner, I must keep to myself. As if I were a flower upon the table, a witness to all the happenings, unable to speak of any even if I wanted to..."

Keziah was impressed, "Exactly, my dear! But if you have any questions regarding the events of the evening you are to come to me only. No one else, not to the Misses, nor Master Job, not even your kin — no one! Do you understand?"

"Yes."

The two returned to their duties, alongside Jah. They chatted and busied themselves while waited for the men to get home. Keren even picked some fragrant flowers from the bushes alongside the house and arranged them in a vase for a centerpiece on the low table where they would recline on pillows on the floor for this twilight meal. "So I don't forget, Ma'am," she replied to Keziah's delighted questioning look.

When Jah saw the flowers, she exclaimed, "What a thoughtful deed! They will be a pleasant aroma, which will make up for the fact that the food will not be as hot nor as fresh with the lateness of the hour."

Suddenly Cale appeared. Despite his sun-darkened skin, he appeared as white as a ghost, obviously disturbed and stricken. "Cale, what is it?" his mother gasped, moving toward him.

Jah just put her hand to her mouth and sat down. She could tell from his appearance that he brought bad news.

CHAPTER 2

Keren instinctively positioned herself behind the Matriarch. "Mother, please sit. Join us at the table, for I have such grave news that I would be unable to assist any who might faint from it. That goes for you too." He addressed Keren, who quickly grabbed her stool to position it where she had just been standing.

"I don't know where to start…" He sat crossed-legged as the older ladies positioned themselves with legs bent at the knees to their side, forcing them to recline slightly to one side.

"Catch your breath." Jah, with deliberate calmness, poured the lad some wine from a skin on the table.

"Thank you." But without drinking any, he continued, "While I was out in the range…after word had reached me of my invitation to tonight's meeting…the fire from God fell on the field…consuming all except myself." All the women gasped. "I ran back here as fast as I could to tell the Master…"

"Job?" Jah attempted to rise to find her husband.

"Wait! There is more. When I got here, father has just informed him…"

"Kadri is back." And Keziah also tried to leave.

"Mother! Please, let me finish, for there is more, so much more." Contained tears filled the eyes of the strong young man, "I have misspoken. Now please settle down and let me finish all I have to say before anyone leaves, please." The weight of the task, or the grim scene he

9

had just witnessed, or most likely the both, had finally caught up to him. A tear trickled down his cheek. He was exhausted, but he composed himself enough to continue.

"Gilad was here before me..." The women looked at each other puzzled, but said nothing, "He had informed Job, the Sabeans attacked the Northern field, all were slaughtered including the animals, save him. Then I came and shared my gruesome news." He almost lost it at remembering, "Then Eitan..." again the women exchanged looks of astonishment, but said nothing, "... informed Job the Chaldeans raided the camels, massacring all, and he alone escaped." The women gasped again, and Jah tried once more to go to her husband, who no doubt was grieved because of this news. "Please, there is more." The young man began to weep now. Jah stayed; Keziah tried to comfort her son, but he pulled from her violently. "I must finish," he barked, then more gently but still adamantly continued, "I must..." His eyes were full of tears that threatened to fall, "Father was the last of us to arrive...He had just come from Erel's, where all your..." Jah nodded that she understood the rest and to urge him to continue. She wanted to get to Job; he would need her.

Cale took a deep breath, staring at the table to contain the emotions welling up inside of him. He knew that even one added gram of empathy from anyone would send his feelings spilling over...No, he was a man, and they stayed composed until their tasks were done, until they were free to do as they pleased in private. "A wind from the wilderness struck the four corners of the house," his voice trembled as he looked directly at Jah to deliver the fatal blow, "father was the only one..."

Jah looked at him as if he were a snake.

"I'm so sorry..." That was it for him, an unending streak of tears flowed down his stone, otherwise emotionless face. No other sounds came from him.

"No!" in disbelief, then she yelled. "No! Not my babies..." She fell back onto Keziah behind her.

"Come now, let me take you upstairs," Keziah beckoned with sorrow thick in her throat.

"My precious babies, Keziah, my babies," was all Jah could say as she was mindlessly led away by her beloved servant and most cherished friend.

Keziah got to the stairs and looked back, "Where are Job and your father?"

Cale, now trembling with emotion, said, "Job ripped his garments and is shaving his head; father is with him."

"Keren, feed them! I will be back as soon as I get Jah settled.," she addressed the bewildered maiden, "Keren! Come on, I need you right now! I can't be in two places."

"Yes, Ma'am," the girl stammered as the two women disappeared.

Keziah managed to get Jah unrobed and dressed in a sleeping gown with little to no help from Jah herself. The woman had just lost everything. She was completely beside herself. She cried, sobbed, and whimpered, all the while allowing Keziah to do with her whatever she wished.

Keziah, too, was tormented by all the news, but her main focus had to be Jah. If she was not careful, they could lose her along with all else. Keziah knew Jah would need constant watching over. She just hoped that nothing else would happen until they could learn to cope with all of this.

She prayed silently as she rocked Jah to sleep like a babe, "Lord, be with us," her soul cried.

Keren was still beside herself. By muscle memory, she went through the motions of fixing the two hirelings, Eitan and Gilad, along with Cale a plate each. Cale, who was still traumatized and in shock, helped her as best he could.

Once she got them settled, she proceeded to find the Master and Kadri. She found them alright, though she hadn't recognized the Master at first. Kadri immediately tried to intervene with the girl witnessing the Master in his present state. "Naked I came from my mother's womb, and naked I shall return there. The Lord gave, and the Lord has taken away. Blessed be the name of the Lord." Job worshiped.

"Child, leave us," said Kadri standing in front of her to block her view.

"I was just coming to see if you would be of need of any sustenance." She humbled herself, looking down with her back to Job as to not even be tempted to look upon the Master lying prostrate upon the ground. "What do I need to bring or send by one of the other workers for either of you?"

"Nothing, Child. The master is worshiping, and I will join him quietly yet ever-present. If we are in need of anything, I will send word to my wife." Keren wanted to tell him of the happenings of the house, but he continued, "In fact, go and tell her and Jah not to fret, for I will stay with him as long as it takes. I trust you will speak only to Keziah of what I have told you and what you have seen."

"Yes, Sir, to her alone will I speak." Keren turned to the house without ever lifting her head and ran back to the kitchen area. Keziah had not yet returned from upstairs. The two other laborers were passed out under a tree. The light from the open fire cascaded a protective glow about them.

Cale, whom she found sitting back at the table, obviously still struggling to comprehend all that had transpired, was fingering the rim of the yet full glass of wine Jah had poured earlier.

Cale, only aware he was no longer alone, began to reflect, "I grew up with them. And only because I had insisted on not being treated as their equal, but to be sent to the field to work, is why I was not with them tonight." He looked up at her, "When Job ran off all the while tearing his robe, and my father followed him, I knew the unfortunate task of telling the women would be mine."

Keren joined him at the table, kneeling upon her knees while reaching for his arm to comfort him. She said nothing as he continued, "I fear Jah will never forgive me…" He shook his head downward mournfully, then gazed into Keren's deep brown eyes in a desperate plea, "Did you see the look she gave me? She will hate me forever for being the bearer and deliverer of such news."

"No, she will not," his mother compassionately offered as she joined them, "She was reasonably upset about all this, that is all." After a moment, she added, "I trust you have all eaten…" looking at the girl.

Keren jumped to her feet with hands tucked behind her, "Yes, Ma'am, all but Job and Kadri, by whom I was instructed to speak to you alone," the girl looked apologetically at Cale.

"I will gather Eitan and Gilad, who are sleeping under the palm tree. They will be more comfortable in bed, but will, no doubt, not want to be alone, at least not on this night." He rose to leave and trudged away.

"Return here when you have settled them," his mother ordered. He nodded and waved his understanding as he left them alone.

"Come now, what is it...." Keziah was short from all the stress of the evening.

Keren made sure not to take it personally, "I went to check on the Master and Kadri to see if they wanted something to eat, which I had doubts they would, but to offer my assistance. But they did not." She blushed from remembering, "Kadri told me to tell you that you and Jah are not to worry and that he will stay with Job; 'as long as it takes' were his exact words."

"As long as what takes?" Keziah was not on her toes, as she usually was.

"He said the Master was worshiping. And that he would send word to you if they needed anything."

"Okay, I'll go check on them."

"Ma'am...I feel I must warn you..." she hesitated.

"Yes, Child, what is it?" Keziah snapped.

"...the Master is naked..." the girl could not bring herself to raise her head nor even open her eyes. She just stood there waiting, whatever scolding was coming.

Very calm and controlled, Keziah said, "I see. Okay," she flattened down her pristine attire, "then I will wait for them until morning and will busy myself with the Mistress and the house until Kadri can get him refurbished." She exhaled her frustration as she thought out loud, then ordered, "You..." pointing at the girl straight in the face, "are not to leave this house for any reason until Job is decent."

"Yes, Ma'am!" she looked straight into her older woman's eyes as she bobbed her head up and down purposefully, "Now can I fix you a plate? I don't think Cale ate much, but he may if you were to eat with him."

"Have you eaten?"

"No."

"Reheat enough for four. When it is hot enough to eat, make me a plate for Jah."

The girl jumped into action, "I've kept it hot." She returned shortly with a bowl of steamy broth with meat and vegetables sitting on a high-rimmed plate, some unleavened bread on a smaller separate dish, and a cup of warmed ewe's milk from that morning's milking, all balanced on a large wooden tray with handles on each side.

"Thank you," Keziah accepted the tray, "I will attempt to get her to eat, then I will be back." Keziah stood up, looked intently at Keren, and said, "And we will eat with Cale," stressing *we*, then added more conversationally, "You are right, he will eat if he is not alone in doing so."

"I will busy myself in the kitchen until then."

Keziah nodded as she lumbered back up the stairs with the soup.

Just as Keziah expected, Jah was curled in a fetal position in the center of the bed. She was sleeping, but Keziah knew it would only be a matter of time before she would wake again.

Keziah set up a small table near the bed and put an overstuffed woolen mat on the floor, along with a flat cushion for her to sit on. With good reason, she would have to coddle the woman at least for the next few weeks, though this was not an inconvenient duty but a cherished responsibility for Keziah. Keziah had been a much younger woman the last time the Mistress had taken ill and needed her in this way, when, so long ago, Keziah was pregnant. That was when she fell in love with not only the mistress and the master but their Lord as well.

She held onto the silent hope that Keren would be able to step in where needed, just as she had had to do back then. She had to credit the girl: she was on the ball tonight. Keziah just hoped that, for this task, the stamina of both of them would hold when their adrenaline would no longer be feeding them. She would have to talk with the child, help her to understand. They all had lost everyone tonight. Then it dawned on her, all including the child, but excluding her and her immediate blood kin. They still had each other. She thanked God in her heart for that.

Jah moaned, "Job, tell me I dreamt it…"

"Are you hungry?"

"Keziah?" she gasped, bolting up in bed. The realization washed over her as she recounted all that had been told to her moments before. "No! Oh, Keziah…" she cried, and her lachrymose continued.

As gently and as encouraging as she could, as if she were talking with a disgruntled and highly, but reasonably upset small child, Keziah asked, "Would you like some soup — it's nice and warm? And maybe later I will bring you some fig bread? We still have a loaf left..."

And then the wailing began again. Keziah had almost had her; she saw it in Jah's eyes, and as soon as she said it, she wanted so badly to take the words back. Unfortunately for them both, Jah made the connection — fig bread equaled kids. Jah would no longer enjoy the decadent sweet that she had made and sent to them that very day.

Jah sobbed it as Keziah thought it, "I wonder...if they...ever...got the chance...to even taste...the bread.... befo...—" she couldn't finish.

To Keziah's surprise, Jah sipped the soup's broth and nibbled the bread. She felt she couldn't eat anything more substantial, given her nerves. Keziah was grateful to have her consume at least something. Once the broth warmed her stomach, Jah settled into bed and fell fast asleep. Keziah left the remaining bread on the bedside table and went back down to check on the rest of the family.

No one was in the dining area. Keziah could hear splashing as if someone was bathing. She hopefully wished that was Job. Then she continued toward the kitchen, where she found Keren straining to shuffle a large pot of water towards a heavy double curtained door that led to an alcove just outside the kitchen. She had heaved it just inside the closest curtain without moving the inner curtain. Strong hands grabbed its upright handle easily and hoisted it quickly out of sight.

"Job getting a bath, finally?"

"Oh," was a startled reply, "No, Ma'am, Cale…"

"Cale?" Keziah yelled, almost furiously.

As if a secret, Keren whispered, "I had suggested it," pointing to her chest while rubbing her achy back.

"That should be plenty, Keren, thanks," Cale yelled from behind the tapestry.

"Okay!" she yelled back; then she cupped the back of her left hand around the right corner of her mouth as she leaned in and said to Keziah, "To get him to relax…" almost in a whisper too low to hear, "though I had to tell him that he smelled and needed to shower for our dinner with him." Then she shook her hands and head dramatically as if to erase what she had just said, "…which I know was not necessary for either of us to have eaten with him…" and, bobbing her head in encouraging agreement, she completed, "but like I said to relax him…"

"I agree with your handling of the situation…" Keziah was stiff. The girl's overly dramatic gestures irritated her. She did everything she could not to incite such behavior, but all the while, she understood it was just her inexperience and immaturity coming out.

Keren clasped her hands behind her back, awaiting further instruction as to give Keziah the rightful position of the head of the household in the current situation.

Keziah moved to the curtain, turned only halfway toward the lass who was now standing behind her, and ordered, "Go ahead and set the table for us."

Then she added, yelling, "When you have finished — dinner's ready…though don't rush, Son," to the wet but not visible body on the other side of the two-layered curtain.

"Yes, Ma'am, I'll be right in—" he answered with a yawn, which told Keziah that the girl had acted sensibly with her offspring.

It was several minutes later when the three of them finally sat to eat. Luckily for both Keren and Keziah, while they initially prepared the meal, they had the privileged duty of tasting it as well. And though it was coming up to the darkest hour of the night now, they were not famished.

To their delight, both women were right about the strapping young man at the table with them now. Cale ate hardily, even having thirds. The women made an extra effort not to finish before Cale to encourage him to have his fill.

And then, a blood-curdling scream rang out! The women grabbed their chests from the shock. The hearts of all of them were beating rapidly.

"Jah…" Keziah panted, then rushed upstairs.

"I'll go check on Dad and Job," said Cale, heading in the opposite direction from his mother.

Left all alone, the girl sighed, "I'll clean up." Her shoulders drooped, "I guess."

CHAPTER 3

It was hours before Keren saw or heard anything from anyone. She had cleaned the dining and kitchen areas twice and attempted once to lay her head down on the table but to no avail. Now, she was sitting in a chair in the doorway on the Eastern side of the house, faced away from where she had last seen Job, and was watching the sun paint the sky as it was rising high.

In a quiet call from the kitchen, behind her came, "Keren?" Cale whispered again a little louder, "Keren?" Poking his head from the kitchen area, he noticed her silhouette.

When he was close enough, she answered, "Over here," without turning toward him.

"What are you doing?"

"Just sitting here..." she replied with melancholy. Then, as if bitten, "Oh! Is there something I could do for you? You need something?" She continued without letting him answer, "Breakfast! I bet you're hungry...I can cook! Then we could eat. Hopefully, Keziah and Jah, Job and Kadri, Gilad and Eitan will all join us, and we can all eat together..." And, as if he had agreed and confirmed that this would happen, "Oh yay!" she clapped, "It will be wonderful. We will need to bring in some more chairs and a bigger table from somewhere... Do you think you could?" as she entered the kitchen.

Reeling from her rant, Cale asked timidly, "What?"

"Could you find a bigger table and more chairs? So we can all eat together when I get breakfast finished? Ooh!

You could set it up outside, in a picnic-style, and we could eat in the cool morning breeze." She bobbed her head up and down like that was the most wonderful suggestion she had ever had.

He shrugged, still confused, "I guess so…"

"Ooh yay! And find some shade, will ya?"

"Some shade?"

"Yeah, so we don't have the sun blinding us while we eat, silly?"

"Oh, right," he faked a laugh, still unsure.

"Yay!" she squealed as she rushed off all excited about the kitchen.

She was making such a racket once she got started that she didn't notice Keziah rushing to the doorway in a huff, "What do you think you are doing?" She clutched the large wooden beams that framed the arched entrance so that she wouldn't strike the disrespectful maid.

"Making breakfast, so we can all eat together," the delirious girl replied, not skipping a bit nor picking up on the fact that Keziah was furious.

"*Well, stop!*" Keziah barked uncharacteristically; her chest was heaving now. She was so filled with disgruntlement that her breathing was labored.

It made the girl so shocked that she was bewildered. She just stared at Keziah, and Keziah, for the life of her, just stared right back. When it finally dawned on the poor sleep-deprived child that Keziah really wanted her to stop, the most hurt look drained her face.

Before she could say anything, Eitan and Gilad, kind of jovial, burst into the kitchen. They quickly slammed into the wall of tension between the two ladies; then, they dropped their smiles, took an about-face, and went right back out the way they came.

As if tears melted her entire stature, Keren collapsed to the floor.

"Oh, jeez, not you too." Keziah dropped her hands to her side.

Big-eyed and heavily breathing, Cale appeared in the doorway, as Keren turned into a puddle of a girl sobbing upon the floor.

"Humph." Keziah retreated from the room.

Cale followed her with long strides, "Mom, what happened?"

"She's in there banging up a storm, about to wake Jah…without a care in the world…" Keziah waved her hands about to mimic the histrionic ridiculousness of it all, "Then when I got onto her…she just, just stared blankly at me like I had lost *my* mind!"

Cale cautiously, "I don't think she has slept…"

"Don't be silly! Why wouldn't she have slept?" dismissing his attempt to justify Keren's actions.

He held up a figure holding her attention with his eyes to give her pause as he backed back into the kitchen. He gingerly squatted next to the puddled body on the kitchen floor. "Keren?" he quietly coaxed.

She raised her head, eyes puffy and red, still overflowing, "All…I was doing…was trying to do…cook breakfast for everyone…and she…came…in here…and yelled…at me…to stop," she sobbed, "I don't understand, what did I do wrong?" she whined.

"You may have been making too much noise in your excitement..." he scrunched his shoulder and made a gesture with his thumb and index finger as he winked in the space between for emphasis.

Her cheeks flushed with the shame of her folly, "Oh..." as she reverted into the emotional quagmire upon the floor.

Careful not to make her notice, Cale got up to rejoin his mother in the next room. He prayed his mother had stayed to see the pitiful sight herself.

"Mom?" he whispered.

He found her standing in a corner, shoulders heaving. "Mama?"

She turned to face him with red, teary eyes of her own now, "The poor child, she...I...what should we do?" she resigned.

"Let her have her breakfast. Gilad and Eitan were looking forward to eating something. I'll eat with them, and we can make plates for you and the rest." He held gently to her upper arms, "You and Dad need to get together and chat." She didn't miss the fact that her son had grown to be a compassionate man. "Let me handle things here, and you go to him by the barn if you can spare a moment away from Jah."

"Cale, the girl needs sleep..."

"Yeah, I haven't figured that out yet, but I do know she really wants to do this, and she's really excited about doing it."

"Okay," she placed her hand in the middle of his firm chest as if bestowing this privilege to him, "You be sure to supervise, though. Don't leave her alone. And afterward, we will think of a way to get her to sleep if a full tummy doesn't knock her out."

"Deal!" he nodded his head once in agreement.

They went their separate ways. Cale returned to the kitchen, and Keziah walked outside to find her soul mate.

She missed him. Though she had slept comfortably in Job's uninhabited bed next to Jah's, it wasn't their bed, with Kadri's arms around her. It was the first time they had spent an entire night without each other in years. Keziah turned the corner around the barn just as she remembered the girl's warning about the master. To her relief, Kadri had talked him into a sackcloth by now, which was understandably covered in ash. She lingered back, waiting to be noticed by her husband; she didn't want to disturb.

At first, he thought it was the maid-servant again. He rose, concerned and eager. He was a few yards from Keziah, and his heart skipped. It was his lover, he had missed her sorely, and the pain caused by their separation grew with every step. He clutched her arm, dragging her back around the corner. Her astonishment reminded him of a time when he happened upon an unexpected doe.

Initially, she thought he would scold her for some reason because of the way he grabbed her. Soon his mouth covered her gaping one, causing her heart to leap with delight. He embraced her with such passion and longing, drawing her ever so closely in a kiss which she would never forget.

A lump caught in his throat, and a tear was in her eye when they finally stepped only inches apart. "I love you!" they both sang in unison. They smiled at each other.

Quickly wiping the tear, Kadri asked, "How's Jah? Cale seems to think she will hate him forever. I hate that he had to be the one to break the news to you."

"No, it was fine. Job needed you. Jah is distraught, to say the least. And she needs me and is going to need me for some time," she announced with the slightest taint of regret in her voice.

"Same here, I'm afraid."

"Well, that's good; at least we both will be doing the same thing, unfortunately just not together."

He kissed her forehead; he loved her for always seeking the silver lining of any situation. "Job has released all the workers, including us," he pressed his lips more firmly to her head, holding her to where she could not change their current positions.

"I can't leave her, Kadri." All she could see of him was his Adam's apple.

"I know, nor can I, but if he insists..." his voice trailed helplessly; he loosened his grip so she could look into his eyes.

"We'll do what we should. Have you told the others?"

"No, not yet. I'm hoping Job will change his mind at least about us."

"The girl servant, Keren, is cooking breakfast; maybe you should join the rest when they eat and tell them then."

"You will not be joining them?" he wasn't happy with this, "You need to eat too..."

"I am," she nodded, "just not with them. Cale is helping Keren. We will make plates for Jah and me. Is Job fasting?"

"Yes..."

"And you?" he could see her calculating everything as he answered.

"Yes, but I will make an appearance," he resigned, "to tell the others."

"Okay, I'll let Cale know so he can fetch you when it's all done."

He pulled her to him again, their eyes locked, uniting their hearts, "Love me…"

"Always…you?"

He kissed her to confirm he did. Finally and almost savagely, he ripped himself from her and walked away. A lump formed in her throat; her arms instinctively reached out after him to beckon him back to their embraces. He never looked back. She turned slowly about toward the house and went back to her duties.

On the way, she decided that the most assured way to get the girl to sleep was to drug her. Something she was contemplating to do to Jah as well. She knew exactly how to execute this plot.

When she stepped into the kitchen, she got a timid look from Keren, who, obviously, was making painstaking efforts to be as quiet as humanly possible. "Sorry, Keren, I had a rough night with Jah, and I'm exhausted. I was going to make a tonic to boost my energy. You want me to make you one too?"

Cale almost hit the floor…his chin did. Luckily, the girl didn't notice, "That would be great! My Granny taught me the recipe of a tonic to put someone to sleep; I didn't know there was one to help you stay awake too."

"Oh, well…" Keziah fumbled with her apron strings, "will you go out to the Western side of the house and pick me some more purple flowers you found there yesterday? And I'll get started. Cale and I can handle things in here till you return."

As if just pardoned from life without parole, Keren jumped up, "Okay! It will be great to get some fresh air." Then she paused with an open basket hugged to her chest, "I take it, Job is decent, finally," as a way of making sure she had no reason not to go outside.

"He is covered…but I wouldn't necessarily say decent."

Keren just grinned as she skipped outside to the freedom she was longing for.

Cale whispered, "Mother!" almost too loudly, "What are you doing? We're supposed…"

"Shhhhh…" Keziah interrupted him, twisting her body so her eyes could watch as the younger lady twirled around the corner of the house and out of sight. She grabbed his shirt to pull his face closer to hers. "I'm making her and Jah the same sleep tonic her granny taught her." Then releasing him, "Hopefully, her grandmother used dried lavender, and I will be able to convince Keren that using fresh is all the difference." She peered out again to keep track of her. "Though the freshness just makes a less potent brew," she said while taking down a pot. "But I will add a little of that," Keziah grabbed a small vile from a high shelf, "and this," taking a bottle of something from another shelf, "and some of this." She added them to the pot with some water and said to her son, "Hurry, go put this on to boil!" as she reached for the tea kettle.

"Ah, okay…" A light bulb of relief went off. He did as instructed, "You want me to help with the ruse? Tell her I often use it in the fields?"

"Only if I prompt you; otherwise, let me handle this, okay?" Keziah began to twist the rag she had just used to clean up a spill she had made, which was rather unusual of her, "I hadn't realized she had knowledge of herbalism, or I wouldn't have tried this ruse at all."

Cale could see her having second thoughts, "Let's just hope it's a very limited knowledge."

"Exactly— " The girl was back already, so Keziah corrected quickly, with feigned enthusiasm, "Exactly, what are we cooking this morning?"

"Slices of cured sheep with leftover fig bread and cheese and milk, along with honeyed fruit," Keren proudly announced.

"Ooh, sounds delightful," Keziah was trying with all she could to control her voice so Keren wouldn't see how fake she was being. "I will have to retreat back upstairs to Jah, but I want to take some to her and eat with her there. I was just telling Cale he will need to go fetch his father when it's all ready." She prayed that Cale caught on. She had only rused someone (meaning their respective husbands) with assistance from Jah a couple of times, and each time she was assisting Jah.

"Right," was all he offered, which confirmed that he understood as he left to fetch another pot.

"You know Granny, too, used lavender in her tonic, along with some spirits?"

"Really? Was it fresh or dried?"

"Dried."

"Ah, yes, I too have used a similar recipe for a sleep aid. But this has fresh lavender, and it is no strong drink. You brew it like tea and add plenty of honey, which revs you right up." Keziah felt ridiculous as she moved her bent at the elbow arms in small circles at her side as if she was running without actually going anywhere.

"Neat, how that works…" Keren touched her chin and looked in the distance, "the same plant used for opposite things like that," pointing at two invisible objects in the air with the same finger.

"Yep! The difference is if the plant is alive or not." Just then, Keziah tossed the fresh herbs into a steamy pot with water and began covering the herb, made by nature to calm, with lots of honey. She strained the brew into the small earthen kettle

CHAPTER 4

Meanwhile, Jah awoke all alone. Her aching heart told her that the past few hours had not been some horrid nightmare of illusions. Silently, the tears streamed down her face into her already damp pillow, which further attested to the truth.

She attempted to rise and find someone, anyone. But the solid door was locked from the outside, which ultimately justified the terrible reality. She climbed into her husband's bed, and at the same time, she got the notion that it was all his fault somehow. He hadn't prayed right, at the right time, with a pure heart...He assured her that he needed to be heard by the God that wasn't ever seen or heard from, but who somehow always heard the purest of prayers.

Then, almost instantly and simultaneously to that thought came, *What if there is not an all-powerful being watching out for us all?* Disillusioned, Jah admitted to herself that she never in her heart truly believed it herself. She only went along with all the ritualistic jargon because Job was the man of the house, her husband, and it was a wife's duty to follow whatever a husband says is right, no matter how ridiculous. Besides, it had never hurt nor failed for that matter until... until last night. But now, this has been proven. "There is no God!" the voice that spoke these words, that came from her mouth, sounded unfamiliar. Her thoughts continued, *How could there be if He allowed such to happen? If there were a God at all, He was not good at all. To destroy so much, so many, in one day, and for what? What was the point?*

She rose from the bed to lay back down on her own. *Why ever allow me to be the happy mother that I had been to steal my children from me? What had the children ever done to deserve their fate? Nothing! So it all had to be Job's fault! Or his stupid god! Both.*

"Now, let me get this right. You want me to wrap this bread in cloth then put it in the fire?" Cale, looking bewildered, was ordered around by Keren as if he was the only hired hand in the room and she, his master.

"Almost. Wrap the bread in this damp cloth. Then, put it in this," Keren handed him an oblong pottery dish, "and place the lid on top; it's over there." She pointed to a full baker's shelf. "Then, put it all into the fire."

"Why wrap it?" Keziah asked.

"Another one of Granny's tricks, it makes the bread soft again, like it was freshly made."

"Oh well, that Granny of yours was a clever woman."

"I hope Jah won't mind us using the last of the fig bread for breakfast this morning."

"Uhh, no, she won't. In fact, let's make sure we use it all up, but don't put any on our plates. She still has the bread from last night upstairs."

Everything was almost ready by now. Keziah got down a tablecloth from an overhead shelf. "Why don't you go set the table with this? I would send one of the boys, but they wouldn't get it straight. And Cale and I will finish up here. Get Eitan and Gilad to help tote all this out for you. That way, they will be doing all the leg work and you — the brain work."

"Okay, sounds great," the girl yawned.

"One more thing, we need to take the tonic."

"So, why don't we just go ahead right now?" Keren suggested.

Oops, now what? Keziah was inventive, "Well, it's best to sip it while you eat. That way, it works with the food to energize you and doesn't upset your stomach. I'll make us both a glass. I'll take mine upstairs with Jah, and you can have yours outside."

"I wouldn't give any to Jah — she should probably sleep as much as possible to heal her broken heart."

"So right, I wasn't going to give her any. She will need milk like the rest."

"Should I go get Dad, now?" interrupted Cale.

"Not just yet, wait till everything is ready. And he and Job are fasting."

"Oh, so why get him at all then?" the girl asked disappointingly.

Keziah, taking into consideration the sleep-deprived girl before her, replied, "Well, he is over everything while Job is in solitude...He will speak for Job regarding what all of us are to do while the Master and Mistress are in mourning."

"Oh, well, aren't we all in mourning?"

"Yes, but there are duties that are still to be done."

"Very true," with that, the girl left.

Both Cale and his mother breathed a sigh of relief. Seconds passed, and the other two servants entered, gathered armfuls of food, and followed Keren to the picnic area they had set up.

Once they were alone, Keziah instructed Cale, "Okay, so when she first drinks this, she may be very energetic.

Don't worry; it won't last. Take her for a walk, but don't leave her alone. You will have to make sure that she gets back to — where should we put her to sleep?"

Eitan entered for another load of food. The mother and son paused their conversation, which gave them both a moment to think. Eitan went about his task in silence and then left.

"How about her bed? Job is covered now," as if they had not been interrupted.

"I just don't want that to trigger an adverse reaction for her losing her people."

Gilad came in and got a load, "Keren and you have done a wonderful job on breakfast."

"Now Gilad, you haven't been sneaking tastes, have you?" Keziah teased.

"Oh no, Ma'am." he returned honestly, "If it tastes anything as it smells, it will be wonderful, I meant." The three of them laughed with delight, and the man left again.

"I don't think it will." Picking up where they left off, Cale explained, "They weren't very close. She and I have spent all morning together. She has told me all about them and hasn't shed a single tear for them. Who we thought was her mom was her aunt. And the man was just a recent boyfriend the woman had picked up. Her mom died, giving her life. In some way, she feels relief from them not being here."

"I always felt uneasy about them. Only because Gilad vouched for them, they had been allowed to stay."

"Yeah, Gilad had known her aunt, but she didn't know anything about Gilad, though."

"I still don't think it would be good to leave her alone right now. She needs to get some sleep first before having to deal with personal emotional stuff."

"Okay, then how about my bed? I'll get her all tucked in and piddle around our quarters until she wakes up?"

Both Eitan and Gilad entered to get the last of the meal fixings. "We can't wait to try all this great smelling food."

"Me either…" Cale agreed with a big grin to his friend, "It's gonna be better than field rations any day."

"Anything is better than the three-day-old bread I was eating in the field, even the soup from last night, which I can't remember even tasting, was better…" The three men laughed.

"You didn't like the stew last night?" Keziah was hurt — that was her recipe.

"Oh…Kay…no, I just couldn't tell you what it tasted like on account of how tired I was…promise!" after an awkward moment, the man went on, "I know it had to have been good cause we ain't having any for breakfast… cause it's all ate up, right?"

"No, there's still some left," Cale whispered.

The color drained from both the minor servants' faces from the embarrassment of the situation.

"You can have some more for lunch later." Keziah offered, "Maybe this time, you will be able to taste it." She couldn't keep her composure. She had to laugh at his expression of the total loss of how to react, "Or you can always forge for some field rations."

"Oh yes, ma'am, it will be our pleasure," he stammered as they left for the last time with the decorated dishware that Keziah allowed to use despite the lack of a special occasion.

Then back to their private, more important conversation. "That will work. Though right after you get Keren settled, you should be free to do whatever for a while; I agree someone should be there when she revives."

"Okay, then that's what we will do."

Keren came inside; she had dark circles under her eyes from lack of sleep. "Everything's set up, would you like me to help you get things set up upstairs?"

"Thanks, but no. I can manage." Keziah smiled. "Don't forget to let your dad know." She reminded Cale.

The young man left to find his father. He was still keeping vigil next to Job. Cale made a bird calling sound. Kadri rose ever so quietly.

"Son," they embraced, "how are your mother and Jah?"

"As expected. Mom sent me to fetch you for breakfast."

"Ahh, yes, the little girl and her big ideas."

"She's been sleep deprived, Dad, and she ain't that little."

"Oh yeah?" Kadri said with a glimmer in his eye.

"Dad!" Cale rolled his eyes.

There was an ever slight change in Job. If Kadri had not shifted his attention, Cale would not have noticed, "I'll be there in just a moment," distracted, Kadri waved his son on.

Cale rejoined the others just as they were all getting settled. All three men went to go for the feast displayed before them.

Keren cleared her throat, annoyed, "I believe Job would give thanks first," she eyed, "Cale?" and bowed her head as she saw the others had done at lunch the day before. The three other slaves looked bewildered at each other; then bowed their heads as well. Kadri said from behind the girl, "God of Job, bless this food and the hands that prepared it. And restore our master's house."

Cale replied, "Amen," and the rest followed in unison.

"Please, come join us." Keren insisted.

"I can't stay."

"At least let me make a plate to take back for you and the master."

"No need." Kadri shook his head, "I need to speak with you all. Job has released us from our duties. If any of you wish to leave, feel free."

"No!" they all voiced their protest.

"Listen! I don't like this any more than you. He has released us as well." The rest settled into the seriousness of the matter. "I think the best thing for all of us to do is to go out and tell the relatives of the deceased that their loved ones are no longer alive. Eitan, Gilad, will you go out the furthest and then work your way back this way?"

"Dad? That's not fair. I'll go too," as humbly as anyone could be, Cale offered.

"Your mother will need you to be close," Eitan answered.

Gilad shook his head mournfully in agreement, "We'll go."

Keren had tears pouring from her eyes, down her cheeks, and into the full plate in front of her. "What about me?" she was barely audible.

"Child, you are home. None of us are leaving. Not for long, anyway." Eitan reassured her as a consoling grandfather would.

"Cale and I will take on the task of telling those closest around us the devastating news. We will have to take shifts in leaving, though. I don't want the women, nor the master left unattended for long."

"Agreed."

"When you go to someone's hearth with the news, make sure you tell them you are 'of the house of Job' and have been sent to inform all of the events here. And you two," Kadri addressed the two older men seated, "when you get back this way, and people are no longer shocked by your news, then you know you have told all you could and should return, as quick as Job's God will allow you."

"As you say, we will do," all the men agreed.

"With all that settled," Kadri lifted the glass prepared for him high, "May Job's God guide us all as we should go," and poured out the goblet as an offering. Then turned to Keren, "And as for you young Lady, you are to keep up all your good works. Cooking like this can only speed things getting back as they should be."

Keren blushed at the compliment and was going to share the glory with her co-cook, Cale, but then thought against it, *After all, cooking is not a manly chore, and it would not bring him the honor it brought me.*

"Okay, then all eat, drink, get some well-needed rest, all of you." Kadri got two inches from Keren's face, "Then be about your duties," and he left.

Keren was trying with all her might to be a good hostess and stay awake at the table.

"Ms. Keren, we'll clean up." Eitan nodded toward Gilad. "It would be our pleasure. Cale, you find her a quiet place to rest, will ya."

Cale, before Keren could even answer in protest, swept her from the table. It wasn't until she noticed that the curtains matched Kadri's robe that she had admired when she realized where she was. "Cale!" she was astonished, "What do you think you are doing?"

Sheepishly innocent, he replied, "Following orders that you get some well-deserved sleep, peacefully and as quietly as possible?"

"I have a home and a bed in it of my very own, thank you!"

He thought she was so cute when she was needlessly offended.

"Then why didn't you go there last night and rest when all else were slumbering, save Job and my Dad?"

"Because I was told not to leave the main house for any reason until Job was clothed, which, as far as I know, didn't happen until some time this morning!"

"Oh! Well, in that case, I'll walk you to your bed, my lady, and will leave you there to rest. I only offered mine cause I thought you couldn't bear going to your own empty, lonely abode."

"Don't bother...I'm a big girl and have been taking care of myself for quite some time now."

He was tired of her attitude now. "*Fine!*" He opened the flap wide so she could pass under it.

She stormed out.

"Keren? Is everything okay?" Cale's mother called after the girl when she stepped into her home.

"Mom, before you say anything, let me explain." Keziah nodded silently with a twinkle in her eye. "I did all as we had decided. I took her here to let her sleep, and she blows up at me," gesturing after her. "However, I did learn why she didn't go to her home last night. She was told not to until Job was clothed, it seems."

Keziah busted into hysteria, "Yes, I'm the one who told her that…"

"Great, a guy tries to be nice and becomes a fool."

"No, dear, I was listening at the door," still laughing, Keziah added. "When I heard you yell back at her, you confirmed why I came out here."

He stared at her, not amused. "She had almost caught me, so I have to address her." She offered, "Get some sleep, Son. You, too, are tired." She kissed him on the cheek and left to go, then turned back. "When you awake, go check up on the girl. You can make up then," she giggled.

He grumbled something inaudible and plopped his face upon the bed.

Jah was still locked in her room. She, the mistress of the house, locked in like a prisoner! She was fuming and getting hotter by the second.

She knew exactly whose fault it was. "Keziah!" she hissed out loud. Keziah was always too controlling and busy for her own good. It wasn't the first time that Jah had been imprisoned in this room by that woman. Just like when she got sick, that one time back when Keziah was carrying

Cale. Job, Keziah, and Kadri (the trio) had claimed that it was for her own good, that they were being threatened by Chaldean raiders. She mocked under her breath, "As sick as you are if they were to raid, you would be defenseless." Then she thought bitterly, "Yeah, bet the only reason I was so weak is because of that witch..." It was a known fact that Keziah knew all about herbs and their uses.

The only difference between then and now was that then they gave her a key to leave at her will, though she never used it. "Where is the key now?" She ransacked her stuff, trying to escape. Countless hair fasteners were now bent and mangled.

Then she heard the key slip into the whole. A flush of panic rushed through her as if she were a child about to be caught with her hand in the cookie jar. She jumped into bed and pulled the covers up over her head, pretending to be asleep.

"Oh, my heavens!" A quiet gasp came from the door, "Jah, what have you been doing?" as Keziah deposited the huge tray containing their breakfast.

"I'll tell you what I've been doing!" Jah pounced from the bed like a lioness attacking her prey. "I've been trying to figure out just when I stopped being the head of this household?"

"Job is still master, m..."

That did it! Jah went off, "Job the master..." she mocked, "Some master, he lost everything...he has nothing left! What, pray to tell, is left for him to master over?"

Keziah was shocked to her core. She had never seen Jah in such a state. She did the only thing she knew. She knelt face first before her owner, surrendering to her will. "Forgive me, my Lady…"

"I'll consider it when you give me the key." Jah barked hatefully.

"Yours is hanging behind your bedpost where it's always been." Keziah was confused and offered Jah the key she used to enter.

Oh, yeah, Jah thought within herself through bittered narrow eyes; she snatched the key offered to her by the woman. *That doesn't matter; she should not have locked me in my room without my permission.* Aloud she yelled, "How dare you lock me in like that! What gave you the right? I am over you, not the other way around!"

Keziah didn't know what to do. Jah has never treated any of her hands like this. Ever! At no time in the twenty-plus years had Keziah been retained by Jah, had she seen this side of the mistress. Much less Jah, treating *her* like this! "Yes, Ma'am." Keziah replied, as humbly as she could, "I brought food for us, but I will leave you to it. May I clean the room, my Lady? Or shall I wait till you have had your fill?"

Jah was feeling a little guilty now. The growing disgust with her own self was almost enough to curb her appetite altogether. "No," she replied, more like a sulking teenager now, then an unappeasable heartless ruler, "come eat."

A table from the corner of the room fit perfectly between the two beds: they could sit upon them and be at just the right height to consume their meal.

Keziah served her friend with love as best she could; Jah seemed to zone out into her mindscape. Keziah wanted to weep but didn't want to get Jah started again. They ate in silence.

Then, without warning, Jah fell straight back on her bed. Her head was hanging slightly over the other side of the full-size bed.

Keziah rose, tidied up the bed around Jah. Then, she moved the table so she could swing Jah's legs onto the bed. Next, she positioned Jah's head comfortably upon her pillow.

Keziah cleaned the rest of the room then went to leave and lock the door behind her, but she no longer possessed a key for that. She clutched the doorknob for support as she silently dried heaved sobs. "I'm not sure how much more any of us can bear," she pleaded from her heart. A feeling of *"this isn't a time to break down"* came over her, as if someone was lifting her up. A strange sense of power and peace came over her, a peace she had never known before. One she could not explain and did not understand. She had this almost euphoric feeling sweep across her as if all was going to be right as rain very soon.

CHAPTER 5

Hours had passed when Cale awoke. He felt as if it were midday. He was hungry again but went to fetch Keren first. He knocked upon the hardwood frame of the shed. No answer. He knocked and spoke loudly, "Keren, you in there?" Again, no response. A streak of panic rose in his throat as he stormed in, yelling, "Keren? Come on, Keren, where are you?"

He looked everywhere — no one, nothing, anywhere.

Cale erupted from the very humble abode and rushed straight for his mother. "Mom! Mom!? *Mom?*" He rounded the corner of the house to find his mother and Keren, laughing like two old friends. He stood in the doorway, mouth agape.

"Cale, you okay?" Keren sang.

"What? Oh yeah, yeah, I'm okay," he seemed haggard.

Keren looked questioningly at him as she turned to leave the room, "Good, hope you're hungry. Your mom and I have been cooking up a storm." Almost in a whisper, "I haven't had this much fun cooking since Granny died. Your mom's wonderful." And she left to prepare the small table.

Once she was out of sight, Keziah repeated the question, "You sure you're okay, Son?"

"Yes, besides the mini-heart squeezes in my chest, I'm fine." He grabbed the counter to stable himself, "I went to her quarters like you had told me to, to find it completely bare!" His skin color was turning back to normal as his mother's face was reddening from trying to hold in her amusement. He glanced at her, then took a double-take. "What?" annoyed, Cale questioned her.

"Oh, nothing…you'll find out soon enough. You both will."Keren returned, humming. Keziah shot her son a look that told him to drop their current conversation. "So, have Gilad and Eitan left yet?" asked Cale as to follow his mother's unspoken orders and change the subject.

"Some time ago…" Keren laughed.

"Your dad wants us to eat inside, and he will be joining us." Keziah radiated with hope, "I have a feeling something has happened to Job that Kadri needs to share; I just aspire it's good news."

"How's Jah?"

Keziah stiffened slightly, "Okay…" Cale could tell something was nagging his mother, "she may be joining us."

"She's up to that?"

"It will be her choice; she is the mistress. Whatever is her will to do, she will do. Only Job has authority over her," she rightly stated.

"I know, but…"

Keziah looked at her son so pitifully that he hadn't the heart to press the subject any further despite the many questions swirling within him.

Then almost startling, Keziah expressed, "I need to speak with your father! If Jah comes down, please be as humble and respectful as you possibly can be toward her." Then as if escaping, she dashed from the house in pursuit of her lover.

Again she lingered by the barn until noticed, which took less time now. As soon as Kadri saw her, he started toward her. She backed herself around the barn corner and went inside to wait for him to join her.

He was almost uncertain of whether she had actually been there or not. Yet he searched her out like a hunter.

"Babe?" he was temporarily blinded by the contrast as he stepped from the sunny yard into the shadowy barn.

She buried her head in his chest and succumbed to the sobbing of her heart. She just wanted him to fix it, though she knew he would not be able to.

"Baby?" he breathed, returning her embrace. He knew this was not a panic cry but a washing of the heart-type of cry. He always hated to see her upset, as this made him feel slightly useless. "Please..." He almost lost it himself, "What is it, my sweet love? Tell me."

Keziah went through the whole spill from when she last unlocked the door until that very second.

Kadri was speechless. He honestly did not know what to do or say. So he shared his news of Job's happenings with his wife as she had shared hers with him.

"Only God can help any of us now."

She agreed, and they both felt the calm after the storm. Yet both were acutely aware the worst was still to come.

"You want to go back to the house? Job will not let me get too close anyway."

"Yes, we have to tell the others, especially Jah."

"Agreed!"

They headed toward the main house. It was eerily quiet. Keziah hastened her step, and Kadri matched her pace.

"Well, it's about time...I was beginning to think you two had deserted the rest of us. But no, your precious child is here; you wouldn't have left him." The bitterness in Jah's voice was undeniable.

Keziah fell prostrate. The youngest of the four servants hesitated only a moment before following suit with Keziah. Kadri attempted to approach Jah humbly with his news of Job.

"Mistress?" he stepped forward.

"No, Kadri." Jah was unfriendly and authoritative, "I'm giving the orders! Not you!"

It caused Cale to join the women in their humbled stance.

"I must tell you about Job..." Kadri, too, joined the others but stayed on his knees.

"*No!*" she screamed, forcing him to lay flat like the others. No one dared look up, "*I am the one in charge, and you all will listen to me and do as I say!*" Then, as if an afterthought, "We will eat. Then I will tell you what each of you is to do. Then if I feel like listening, I will hear what you have to say." Still, no one moved. "You..." they all looked at once to see to whom she was addressing, "Kerreen," she snarled, "you will serve. Cale, get an extra chair. The two turtle doves can clean up after the meal...*Child*, come seat me!" she ordered them.

They all sat stiffly as Keren dished out each platter. Then Jah just dug in without another word or glance.

The four hired hands looked at each other bewildered. In unison, they all bowed their heads to pray.

"Oh, no! We are not doing anything of the sort anymore! There is no need to pay homage to a ruthless god. I refuse and will not allow it!"

Keziah was too busy crying with no sound to take a bit. Had she opened her mouth, she would have wailed. The others just picked at their meal.

Jah could feel the bile back up in her throat. What was she doing?

"Okay, Kadri, what is it?" asked Jah, sounding like the woman they all knew and loved.

"I don't know how too…"

"Just spit it out!" she snapped impatiently.

"He has boils," he said dryly.

The others gasped.

"What?" she asked.

"All over his body, from head to toe…I pray he survives."

"I told you none of that!" Then she leaped from the table, charging out to Job.

When she had gone, both women burst into tears. Consequently, both men reached to embrace the one closest to his age.

"What has gotten into her?" Cale was still reeling.

His father just shook his head, not knowing.

"I fear the answer to that very question." His mother offered through sobs.

Outside, Jah stormed up to her husband, "Do you still hold your integrity of believing in your God?" She looked upon him with disgust, "Why don't you just curse God and die?" she hissed.

Job vaulted toward her. It was obvious that he was making painstaking efforts to not touch her. "You are talking like a foolish woman." wide-eyed he had startled her, "Shall we accept only good from God and not trouble?

"He was a frightful sight. Tears welled up in her eyes, and she fled from his presence. She could no longer stomach herself. She vomited just outside the kitchen door before reentering the house and heading straight for the stairs.

All the servants saw was a blur rushing past, and then they heard the bedroom door slam shut.

Keziah looked at Kadri apologetically.

"You know she locked it," he answered her unspoken plea. Again she gave him a look of earnestness.

"Go...I'm not saying you shouldn't go. I'm just making sure you know what you are going to find once you get there."

She kissed his cheek and went after her friend. Her husband was right: the door was locked. She knocked."

Go away!" a banshee sounding voice emitted from beyond the door.

"I can't..." Keziah admitted, then slid down the floor. Keziah cried while her heart pleaded to God for relief to their aching souls.

CHAPTER 6

The next morning, both Cale and Kadri headed out to inform those close to them of the tragedy. Neither of them wanted to go, but it was mutual between them that this was the best way. They both were drawn to this decision.

Keren knelt down beside Keziah, "Keziah, the men are leaving. I'll stay if you would like to go and tell them goodbye."

"What...leaving?"

"Yes, they want to hurry and go tell the families of the deceased of their losses. They know they will cover more ground quicker if they both leave in opposite directions."

Keziah still looked confused.

"I'll stay here if you want me to, so you can go."

"No, that won't be necessary."

Both women picked themselves off the cool landing just outside the master's bedroom and headed out to see the men off.

Keren approached Kadri first while Keziah went to her son.

"Y'all, please be careful," she urged.

"I don't know if I should tell you to try to keep the peace or stay out of their ways. Either way, we all need lots of guidance from the heavenly One."

"I will try to pray to Job's God too like Cale has taught me."

They gave each other a very platonic embrace.

"Mom, don't cry," Cale hugged his mother.

"When did you decide this?"

"Last night, when you disappeared after Jah."

She exhaled her surrender, "I love you, Son, be careful." She wanted to tell him to take care of his father but knew they would not stay together as they traveled.

Then, they all switched. Keren went to Cale and Keziah to Kadri.

"I wouldn't blame you if you wanted to leave too," Cale said sheepishly.

"Oh no, I believe you both; leaving is right, but I don't think I should." Keren pointed to her chest and shook her head in an honest reply.

Keziah tried not to cry as hard as she could. She was holding her breath when her husband embraced her with his big, strong, safe-feeling arms.

"We'll be back as quick as God allows."

She just nodded her understanding. Kadri rubbed her back for comfort. She wrapped her arms around his waist, nestling in his hold.

He had to do something to get her to laugh so he could kiss her goodbye. He couldn't leave her without one last kiss. "You girls don't go killing each other nor tearing down the house while we're gone," he grasped Keziah's shoulders and pulled her away from him so she could see the humor on his face. "Hear me?" he shook her shoulders for emphasis.

She blushed, smiled, rolled her eyes, and tucked her head back under his chin onto his chest.

"Oh, how I love you, woman."

In response, she tipped-toed to kiss his neck just at the jawline. He hugged her and spun them around to turn his back to the others dipping her slightly. He kissed her mouth passionately and deeply. Both drew from the other strength, which seemed to energize them, not depleting either of them.

"I guess I'm just hoping you'll still be here when I get back." Cale kicked at the dirt under his feet. He couldn't bring himself to look up. There was this strange fear that the girl would see right through him, and considering that he wasn't exactly sure of what this was, he knew his heart couldn't stand her rejecting him.

"I will..." she looked at him so assured as if his sentiment was a silly one. "I'll be right here when you get back," pointing to the ground in front of her, then directly to him.

They just stood there quietly together, not knowing what else to do or say.

"Alright, Son, we'd better get going. Come give your momma a hug."

He did, and she kissed his cheek.

Kadri moved to squeeze Keren's shoulders. "He'll be back soon..."

The couples switched one last time; the older two pressed their lips together in a quick yet meaningful kiss.

"Oh yeah! Here." Kadri held out a small key identical to the one Keziah had relinquished to Jah.

The younger two held each other's elbows at arm's length. Cale looked intently into Keren's big brown eyes, "I'll miss you." He jerked her to him for a quick kiss on the lips, then walked away without looking at anyone.

It happened so quickly that hardly anyone even knew it did, including Keren.

The two women stepped closer to one another, holding onto each other as if holding onto their only lifeline.

As the men headed off in the distance, Keziah leaned to Keren and whispered, "Has my son just done what I think he has?"

The younger female whispered back to the older one, still dazed, "I'm not sure…"

Jah was distraught. She was angry and hopeless. She didn't know what to think or what to believe. She just wanted it all to go away. The humiliation, shame, and guilt; they all were so unbearable.

She rose from her bed and set on Job's. The accusing look in Job's eyes was haunting her. All night she had delusions of hatred in those eyes that once loved her so completely. All of her past sins against him piled before her. Her whole being ached and mourned and needed relief from the stress.

She felt as if she were going mad. She just wanted it to stop, to go away, to leave her alone, to end. She sprang from her bed and ran, smacking into the window frame and knocking herself out cold. Glass fell outside the window when she bounced off of it and fell back onto the floor, bumping the back of her head with a thud.

The two ladies outside heard the sound of the breaking glass and took off running. Instinctively, Keziah ran toward the house; by default, Keren headed towards Job.

"Are you okay, Sir?" Keren heaved.

Crouched before her in ash, awkwardly waving her off from behind himself was a dim reflection of the man she knew to be her Master. Without turning towards her, he looked at her over his shoulder with a half-embarrassed, half-offended snarl.

The view startled her to complete silence. All she could do was turn her body as she stared at Job. Once she had turned so far, and her head had no choice but to tear her eyes from the gaze, she quickly snapped her head around to face forward and bolted for the house.

She clung to the countertop to braise herself as she tried to erase the morbid scene from her mind. Once she could open her eyes and not see his face, she cautiously turned towards the stairway. Then she heard what sounded like somebody was slamming a door, which jolted her into action again.

Once in the upstairs doorway, she found Keziah trying to lift Jah, a much bigger person than herself, off the floor. The girl gasped when she saw a bright red stain covering the front of Keziah's blouse as she shifted the woman, trying to get a good grip on her.

"Well, don't just stand there; help me get her to the bed."

Keren headed to Jah's feet. Once there, she saw the gruesome sight of Jah: her entire head was covered in blood. "She's bleeding!" she squealed as she grabbed the lower half of the woman and pulled it with all her might.

"Yeah, I know. The problem is I don't know from where, the front or back."

Between the two of them, they got the dead limp body on the bed. Keren rushed out of the room to fetch clean water and rags, while Keziah took an unstained piece of her skirt to wipe away the crimson moisture from the woman's face. She could see several scratches, some deeper than others, here and there on Jah's beautiful, full face.

She was lifting her head to assess the back of the head when the child reentered the room with full arms. Keren set everything down on the table as quickly as possible. Then she took about half of the rags she had and submerged them in the water. She pulled them out, ringing them as she did, and plopped them on the bed. Then, she picked one and wrung it out a little better, and began cleaning the face of the woman who was lying horizontally.

Keziah reached across and got one of the rags to clean the back of the head.

"Keziah, she looks dead…is she dead, Keziah?" the girl asked in a panic.

"She's not dead! We need to apply pressure to cut off the blood." Keziah reassured her, overly calm to ease the girl so that she could stay focused. Both women had one hand on Jah's face, ensuring the airflow, and the other on the back of her head, squeezing with all their strength. When the rag was full of blood, only one of them would let go, long enough to toss that rag on the floor and grab the next dry one.

Finally, grabbing for the last clean towel, Keziah saw less red and more white on the rag when they pulled it from the scalp to check it. She knocked the soaked pillow on the floor and nodded at the other bed. The girl half-turned and snatched the other pillow and placed it quickly where the other had been.

"How do we keep it from starting up again?" Keren pondered.

"There!" Keziah pointed behind the girl. "The belt there."

At the end of Job's bed was the braided cloth belt Jah had made him for their wedding day. Keziah carefully pressed the last clean cloth to the back of Jah's matted hair. Then she wrapped the belt around Jah's face several times to secure it while making sure the cloth belt also covered the scraps around the face. Jah looked like a newly wrapped mummy. After that, both women washed off in the water pot; Keren tossed the stained water out the broken window. Keziah stripped her shirt from herself, then bent down to pick up all the dirty tatters off the floor.

Keren brought the bowl over for Keziah to deposit them in. "I'll deal with these; you tend to her."

Keziah opened a drawer and fetched a clean shirt, "We mustn't let the sun fall upon the blood, or the stains will never fade."

"Yes, I know. I was going to hide these clothes in the cupboard until nightfall. And fetch some more, in case we need them."

"I have some at my place."

"And I, at mine; I'll get them all."

The older of them nodded her approval as the younger dashed from the room.

By the time Keren finished all her running around, she was exhausted. She took the steps slowly with arms full. When she got to the room, Keziah had rearranged the room so that they would have an easier time getting things from tables in a pinch. Keren placed half of the rags on one table near the windows and the other half closest to the head of Jah's bed in the corner. Keziah had filled pitchers of water that had matching basins underneath.

"Why don't you lay down and rest on Job's bed while I go fix us some lunch?" Keziah suggested.

"Oh no, I couldn't!"

"Why not? He's not using it. Besides, I don't want to leave Jah alone." Keziah knew this was going to be a hard sell, so she pulled out all the stops.

"You sure no one will mind?" Keren yawned and stretched, "I could go make lunch, and you could rest."

"I'll take a nap after lunch. But even if you don't sleep, please stay with her. And if either of you needs anything, just yell for me."

"Okay. Let me know when it's ready."

"I'll bring it up here. I really don't want to leave her alone."

The girl nodded, then laid down, and Keziah left the room.

Keziah made a big pot of chicken soup. She knew it was too much for her and the girl to eat in one sitting, but she had a welling pot that she kept down in the cool water of the well closest to the kitchen. Usually, they stored butter and whey for breakfast there, having fresh milk any other time. But her chicken soup would use up the rest of what was left in the pot. So the pot could hold half of what she cooked, and it would stay good for a few days.

At the well, she pulled up a heavy rope, not the one used for the water pail. An iron pot with a matching lid was tied to its end, and it was secured with two iron rings, each connecting both ends of the rope with a cord. One had a short cord with the ends tied to the opposite sides of the ring; it was just big enough to go around the bottom of the pot with the ring sitting on top of the lid. The other had two cords attached to it: one had both ends tied on the same side and was longer than the other ring's cord. It had to be fed through the other ring, and it too hooped around the bottom of the pot. On the opposite side of this ring, one end of another rope was tied, while its other end was anchored outside the well so the pot wouldn't sink. This setup worked quite well, and it secured the lid onto the pot so nothing could get inside, not even water.

Keziah unharnessed the pot, leaving its rigging near the base of the well. She got the soup going in a slightly bigger pot.

She suddenly had an epiphany. There is no reason for the girl not to sleep well with everyone gone, *I will sleep in Job's bed, and she can have her own bed. I'll get...*Keziah forgot all the men had left. She marched over to Keren's abode. It was humble, to say the least. As with any newcomer, Job had a roof with four corners to hold it up made for them to start a dwelling place. Walls were something the family was responsible for putting up on their own.

The boyfriend of Keren's aunt was known to be lazy. Keren was the one who made the drapes and hung them. She worked every day for a week on it before being asked to help in the kitchen.

As soon as Keziah flipped back the drape from the outside, she was in a bedroom. It was a large yet unkempt area. It had a chest set to the side of a large pallet on the floor. The drapes that covered the makeshift walls were of a different pattern inside. There was an area off to the side of the larger one. She pulled back the curtain; to her relief, the girl had more of a cot than a bed. Her area was much cleaner than the rest.

Cale had told her that the girl had asked for some branches of particular lengths. Keziah was beginning to realize just how handy and crafty this young lady was.

The cot was sturdy but light. Instead of weaving back through the way she came, Keziah untied the flap to the outside closest to Keren's room. She haled the cot to the main house setting it up in the dining area, off to the corner.

Keziah stopped only to tend to the soup; she made several trips to Keren's and back until she was satisfied that Keren would feel at home in the space she had made for her.

When the soup was done, Keziah made two bowls and headed for the stairs. Once by the room, she gently toed the door open, placed the bowls on the table by the windows, then checked on Jah before rousing the child.

"How is she?" Keren, who was still laying down, looked up at the older lady leaning over their mistress.

"She's a little warm, but not dangerously so."

Keren sat up. She noticed the soup. "Smells wonderful," she nodded toward the bowls and went to get up.

"I'll bring it to you." Keziah beat her to them. Keren moved to the head of the bed so Keziah wouldn't have to climb over her to sit.

"I have a surprise for you when we're done."

"Oh?"

"I think you will like it, or I hope you do."

"I'm sure I will…" Keren tried not to rush, but the promised surprise was killing her manners.

Keziah, too, couldn't handle the suspense and ate faster than usual. She handed her empty bowl to Keren, "Let me head down first. I want to see your reaction." Keziah hurried down the steps to look over everything once more. She remembered the steps being hued out by hand by her master and her husband when they were much younger men. Initially, one would have to climb a ladder to reach the natural loft in the rock. But as Jah started having babies, Job started on this endeavor. The start of that project had not only bonded the four of them together but also solidified her love for Job's God. She remembered how she thought his idea was ludicrous until the project was finished. Job kept telling her, "Trust not what you see." Oh, how she was grateful that through the past few days, she did not have to contend with that old ladder now.

Keren gathered the empty dishes, then slowly followed. She was trying to guess what the surprise was. She would have never guessed what she found. Her eyes were wide with delight; she was speechless.

Keziah took their empty bowls, "Get settled. Make sure I got what you will need." Keziah beamed.

"Tha...thank you."

"We're going to need to stay close together. For the best of all of us." Keziah went to the kitchen to wash the dishes. The soup had cooled down enough to transfer most of what was left to the welling pot.

"Keren, can you help me, please."

"Yes, Ma'am. Thanks again." she hugged the older woman.

"Enough of that." Keziah squeezed back, "I need help taking this out to the well."

"Sure, what's in it, mud?" as Keren lifted the heavy pot.

"Leftovers."

"Ah, so we don't have to stop and cook if things are hectic."

"Precisely!"

Once at the well, Keren steadied the pot while Keziah replaced its harness. They lowered the pot gingerly together.

At first, Keziah thought a bug had jumped into her hair and startled back. It was mid-afternoon, and a cool breeze tussled the women's shirts. Then Keziah and Keren both felt several drops hit them. Both looked at each other knowingly and took off for the house. With each step, the rain came harder. They were soaked through and laughing when they reached the kitchen.

"I haven't run like that in years," Keziah said, still laughing and winded.

"Ooh, the rags. This is just what they need." Keren took them from their hiding spot as both women headed back out into the storm toward the clothes rocks.

They spread the rags over the rocks, so the cool downpour washed out the deep red stains. Once the rain stopped, they would dry this way too. Keren made a mental note that she should listen out for the rain to stop to double-check that all the blood was gone.

Keziah unbuttoned the blouse that she had worn earlier to lay it flat out. Keren placed the crimson-stained pillow into the pot that had contained the rags to soak; this too would need further tending to once the monsoon stopped.

"I hope the boys aren't caught in this." Keziah worried.

"What should we do about Job?"

"I'll check on him, but I doubt even this will move him."

"Okay, I'll go check on Jah then." Keren was relieved not to have to see the master again. Not only had he been intimidating before, in control of her fate and even death if he chose so, but now he was also disfigured and scary looking.

By the time Keziah made it back to the house, she was covered in mud. She stopped at the kitchen door and poked her head inside.

The girl was astonished, "My goodness, what happened to you?"

Still standing in the doorway, Keziah replied, "I fell."

"Oh my, are you okay?"

"Yes, just a couple of bruises, my ego included. Will you hand me a lidded pot? I'm going to run to my house and get a change of clothes, and I don't want to get them wet."

"We're gonna need to bring your hope chest over when the rain stops, so you have clothes here too."

"Agreed, but right now, I'll settle for one outfit. Is Jah okay?"

"No change. We can discuss the masters once you're dry."

"Okay, I'll be right back." Keziah took her time: one, she didn't want to fall again, but two — to let the rain wash her clean.

She grabbed a blanket from a shelf right inside the front door so she wouldn't get the whole house wet while she looked for some dry clothes. She gathered everything in the pot with the lid secure, then headed out again, leaving the blanket behind. The rain seemed colder to her this time, which would be good for the linens out on the rocks but not for her old bones. *Lord, see us through and don't let me get sick, please, they all need me.*

CHAPTER 7

What would have taken several days took only two. Both Kadri and his son were back at the manor just before dawn on the third day. They had even informed Job's closest friends of all the happenings.

To keep the stress levels to a manageable level, Kadri often teased Keziah about what "really happened" to Jah that day they left. At first, Keren would defend her. Then Cale saw that she was starting to doubt his mother's integrity. He pulled her off to explain.

"Have you ever seen anyone love another as much as my mom?"

"She definitely is the greatest example I've ever seen of a woman who truly adores her husband immensely."

"Yes, she is, but that's not what I meant," Cale had Keren's undivided attention, "You're right, they love each other totally, and before this tragedy, Job and Jah were their only equals. But I was talking of my mother's love for Jah."

Keren mulled this over while he continued, "Not once will you ever hear my mom say anything negative about her, even when it's undeniable that Jah is in the complete wrong. Take Jah's attitude toward Job — he is the Master of us all, that includes Jah. And she was in the complete wrong when she bad-mouthed him the day after the hand of God took everything from Job because God could have taken her as well. Instead of looking at God's mercy of them having each other, she became a wound in his side. But mom will never say anything bad about her and would be mad at me for even speaking this truth about her because it makes Jah look unfavorably."

Keren furrowed her brow; she was trying to see his point. "I've explained all this to say the following: Dad knows that Mom would never hurt Jah. He is teasing her. Next time he does: let him, don't jump to her defense, but watch closely as they interact."

They returned back to the main house. Jah wasn't running any fever, but she wasn't waking up either. She did respond to the light of the day by thrashing about whenever the sun shone on her. She did not, however, revive otherwise. In response, Keziah covered the window with a thick dark curtain to keep Jah from reopening wounds.

On the fifth day after the accident, three men, friends of Job's, with a small entourage, approached the house. They were still far off when they noticed Job. Kadri went out to meet them.

"Where is your Master?" one spoke to him.

"There." Kadri pointed to the mound of a person upon the ash heap.

The prominent men began weeping, tore off their mantles from about their necks, and threw ash in the air towards heaven. They were clinging to one another, sitting only a small distance from Job, and lamenting silently.

The four landlords stayed this way for seven days and seven nights. Kadri was the only one who ventured anywhere close to them. He never spoke to any of them; he would just come close enough to make his presence known, stay for as long as he felt the need, then return to the house.

During that time, although she never opened her eyes, Jah began speaking. At first, everyone was happy and excited, though no one could understand her. Each was thinking she would be up and about soon. By the second day of the lamentation, Eitan and Gilad were back as well. Gilad had bought a female goat that was milking, some butter, and a few other culinary delights. That night, they had potato soup for dinner with chunked potatoes with milk and butter, the cheese they had stored from three seasons prior, some bitter herbs, and just enough water to drown it all.

So everyone could stay together, the housing arrangements were moved about in and around the main house. Keren had her place over in the far corner across from the kitchen. Kadri and Keziah had the space closest to the Eastern side of the house. The other two, who were used to sleep outside and near the animals in the fields, slept inside the animal keep. They were happy to tend to their guests' animals. Cale took the night shifts of keeping an eye on Jah, sleeping in Job's uninhabited bed. The guests took up what was Kendri and Keziah's, as well as Keren's, abandoned abodes that were the establishments closest to the main house. With all the extra bodies about, it wasn't long before the girls hoisted up the leftover chicken soup from it's cool, watery hiding spot.

For the first few days, those of the House of Job took shifts sitting with Jah. But her ranting was so disturbing for the older men and Keren that by the end of it, only Keziah and Cale could stand to be in her presence. Eventually, the two of them started grasping some of Jah's words, although they did not understand what they meant.

Kadri decided to get everyone back on some kind of schedule. The planting season was here, so the men labored about the grounds, staying away from the distress of the others. The friends of Job's attendants also joined in some of the work, saying it was better than just sitting around idle, which was fortunate since Cale was often needed to help with Jah. The women took care of the main house and Jah.

Then one night, when Cale was sitting with the comatose woman upstairs, after all, had retired for the evening, Keziah seemed distant.

Her husband, thinking he knew why she was so distant, offered in her ear, "Dear, what troubles you so? Job's friends, although they say nothing, are here to help him."

"I know," she responded dryly.

"Then what? What is it?" wondered Kadri, understanding now that what was on his wife's mind had nothing to do with Job.

"Jah…" Keziah looked out into nothing as if watching the scene unfold before her as she spoke. "She was at first mumbling to herself. As if hopeless. Remember, at first, when the sun hit her, Jah screamed as if being tortured or burned." He only nodded, trying to follow her thoughts. "Well, today, when the sun showed on her, for Cale accidentally pulled the draperies down, it seemed like hope ignited in her. Then when I put them back up, her countenance fell deeper than before…"

"Maybe she dreams? And what is happening in reality affects those dreams?"

"Maybe…" Keziah was still troubled.

CHAPTER 8

On the morning of the eighth day after Job's guests had arrived, Keziah was determined to check a hunch. She was eagerly fixing breakfast when Keren found her. "Cale still sleeping?" the girl inquired. "I don't know. I need to make Jah breakfast before I check on him," was the zombie-like answer.

The girl just backed out of the kitchen and went to check on Cale to inform him, the only other coherent person in the house at the time (the men had long gone out to work), of what she was not sure was up with his mother.

Cale approached his mother cautiously, "Mom? What are you doing?"

"Oh good, you're up!" Keziah handed him a platter of food, "Making Jah breakfast; I'm going to wake her up today," she announced confidently.

"Hmmm," Cale was still not sure if his mother was suffering from some delusion. "And how are you going to do that?"

She quickly stepped to the other room and gathered some pillows. She rushed up the stairs. He was fast at her heels. The tray was cumbersome but didn't slow him down.

They entered the room, and he placed the tray on the table. His mother was propping Jah up with more pillows. The whole time he was trying to beckon a response from her, "Mom, answer me...Mom, how are you going to revive her?" He spun her around to face him and kept her from moving. By this time, Kadri was in the room as well. Cale had told the girl to fetch him.

"What's going on?" Kadri sought an answer. "Job and the men are speaking, and I want to be out to hear if they are in need of anything."

"I'm going to wake up Jah." Keziah was looking intently into her son's eyes.

Jah tossed and turned as if fighting to get away. Everyone looked down at her.

The father asked his son the same question he had just moments before downstairs. "How are you going to do that?" Kadri repeated as if her words were an absurd notion.

She wrenched from her son's grasp and headed over to the window directly across from Jah's bed. "By showing her that it's a brand new day." She ripped the curtains wide open, "It's morning. Time to rise and shine like the sun," she demanded.

Keren gasped while the men tensed up. Jah seemed to freeze as the sun bathed over her. Then it was as if she melted into relaxation and contentment. Keziah stepped in the way of the sunlight casting a shadow over Jah's face. Her eyes fluttered open. She looked about the room confused but yet at the same time relieved.

"You hungry?" Keziah floated towards the table to retrieve something from the tray. "I didn't know what you would want, so here is some bread and milk." She sat gingerly on the bed next to her friend. Everyone was astonished and misty-eyed when Jah smiled broadly and thanked her servant graciously.

They almost toppled the table as they stumbled over each other, trying to get it closer so Keziah wouldn't have to walk.

"Oh my! Won't you take part with me?" responded Jah when she saw the bountiful spread.

Kadri kissed her squarely on the forehead, "None for me. Welcome back! I need to check on Job." Before he straightened up completely, he shifted his weight, "I love you, my wonderful wife," and kissed Keziah too, but on the month. He nearly ran over the dumbfounded Keren when heading out the door. He kissed her on the cheek to shock her back into the reality of it all. He placed his hands firmly on her hips and swung the girl around him so they would trade spaces. Then, facing the room, he said to his son, "No kisses for you." and left for outside.

CHAPTER 9

His heart was full of joy as he bounced down the steps and out of the house. He was on such an emotional height at that very second that he thought he could burst from happiness.

Then he rounded the corner of the stable and ran smack into the wall of tension from all the frustration of men arguing. It was such a dramatic contrast of emotion that it quite literally knocked him down to a seated position, legs outstretched in front of him. He was struck, dumbfounded as he listened to them berating back and forth.

The arguing went from one to another, and all the while, Job defended his integrity.

Sometime later, Kadri absently drew his knees up, rested his elbows on top of each corresponding knee, and, with hands clasped in between his knees, rested his head upon his hands. Intently listening, he thought to himself, *If this were any other being that they were so brutally accusing of wrong, then they may have been right.* Still taken aback by it all, *But this is Job and what they were accusing him of is plain wrong.*

The landlords would pause every now and then to collect their thoughts and consider the arguments made. During the first of these, Cale approached his dad, who was still on the ground.

"Dad," in a low, hushed tone, "we have set up in the barn. Eitan and Gilad are in the loft, and you and I can be in the stables area. I've got Keren running between us. I think we should make a record of this."

Despite his age, Kadri rose from seat to feet with little effort, never placing even a hand on the ground. He followed his son, "Great idea."

They worked quickly to get into comfortable positions. Each had a small sharp pick used for whittling details and a large piece of thick bark from when they had stripped a huge oak tree to make Keren's family frame for their tent-like dwelling.

Each man followed the speech of only one of the four landlords. Kadri wrote Job's words, Cale — Eliphaz's, Gilad — Bildad's, and Eitan — Zphar's.

Then, during round two of the debates, Job confirmed that this was what they ought to do. In the midst of one of his rants, he spoke, "Oh, that my words were written! Oh, that they were inscribed in a book." The five servants all prayed with joy that God had positioned them to grant their master's request.

Keren was able to run to the house and refresh fruit and bread, and a water skin for each. She set up a table for all the refreshments, big empty baskets for the written on bark pieces, next to the big pile of bark that had not been written on yet.

The next time the masters took a break from arguing, the servants all convened together and refreshed themselves. Keren expressed, "If any of you need a break but are not able to wait for them to pause, I know how to write."

"Really?" Kadri was impressed.

"Show me." Cale had to see this.

Gilad offered, "Your mom's dad taught you. He had taught your aunt."

"Grandpa taught me and my mom. My aunt never learned." As she sat to write, "Did you catch Job saying he wanted us to do just what we are doing?"

Cale laughed with delight, "Yes, I did. Joy filled my soul."

Eitan, "And mine."

They all nodded.

"Let's get back into position. And if anyone needs to, use Keren." Kadri ushered.

By the end of the third round of the rants, Job's friends had stopped arguing. The four male slaves of Job reconvened while Keren straightened up. Then a younger man, who was part of the entourage, spoke. Keren grabbed a blank piece of bark and a whittler. She copied word for word all he said.

It was past the middle of the day, yet too early for dusk when clouds rolled in and the rude invaders left. Job was speaking out loud…to himself?

One cold drop, and then another hit the ground; a chill went up Kadri's spine.

"Let's get to the house."

No one needed a second word. Everyone grabbed something and followed Kadri.

CHAPTER 10

Meanwhile, Keziah fed Jah, eating with her to encourage her to take plenty of food. It was almost like old times, but there was a slight difference in Jah.

"Keziah, what did Kadri mean by 'check on Job'? What's going on?"

Keziah feared that once Jah revived, she would have some memory loss. Often with tragedy, a mind would forget for the body to survive.

"How much do you remember before you were out?"

"Let's see…I remember…the kids are gone…" her face was grim, "and we have nothing," she stated matter of factly, "and Job has boils…" this sparked her, "Are they worse? Do we need to go to him? Is there anything we can do for him?" she attempted to get out of bed but winced with pain.

Okay, well, maybe she won't have amnesia. "Well, Eliphaz, Bildad, and Zphar showed up about a week ago but haven't spoken to anyone until today. They have been keeping a silent vigil at Job's side since arriving."

"Oh…" Jah sighed with relief, "but nothing has changed with Job?"

"No, Ma'am, not that I know of." Keziah needed to keep Jah busy, but she couldn't be allowed to overexert herself in this room. "Hey, you want to switch to Job's bed so I can freshen up yours?" almost as an afterthought, Keziah touched the older woman's hair, "And we can wash your hair, so when you do go out to see Job, you're all freshened up?"

Jah sensed this was all that Keziah was going to let her do. She agreed. Keziah helped Jah sit on the edge of her bed. That was when she got a glimpse of herself in the reflection of the newly restored blank window when Jah was really grateful that Keziah was going to help her become more presentable.

"What in the world happened to me?"

"You will have to tell me, I'm afraid."

Keziah left to give Jah a chance to collect her thoughts and to get all she would need to change the bedding and give Jah a bath.

"I'm not sure what is real of it and what is just in my head," Jah expressed during one of Keziah's trips from downstairs.

"I should have everything this next trip. Then you can just babble it all out. We can try to sort it all out together." Keziah left again.

Jah tried hard to find a beginning. Keziah helped her off her bed and onto Job's bed. "Oh yes," this triggered her memory, "After Job and I argued, I was in here...alone. I had been so terrible to all of you," her voice was thick with guilt and regret, "to you especially, Keziah, how can you forgive me?"

Keziah had tears fill her eyes; she waved her on as if swatting a fly.

"I'm so sorry."

"I love you...it's fine, continue," she beckoned, swallowing her tears.

"I was wallowing in self-pity. Just beside myself with it. Then everything went black. When I awoke...but I wasn't awake," Jah shook her head.

Keziah had stripped her bed, opened the window, and tossed the linens out. They landed in the wash area off the side of the kitchen.

"Anyway, I was in utter darkness. I could hear two people speaking, but it was muffled."

Keziah tried to make real-life connections to what Jah was saying. *Was that Keren and me speaking outside the door that morning? It couldn't be! She didn't have the accident till the men left, and that was before.* Keziah said nothing, just listened.

"Then I was yanked from what seemed like a box of some sort, but once I was standing, there was nothing there. The place I was in was utterly dreadful: flames everywhere, the smell of cooking rotting flesh, screams of agony. My mouth was so parched; my tongue was swollen. I could barely speak. I asked over and over, 'where am I, what am I doing here?'"

Keziah was done making Jah's bed. She helped her to the chair near the table and undressed her so she could bathe.

Jah just continued, "What do you want with me? I think I asked, or at least wondered if they were Chaldeans or Sabeans, but knew they were far worse."

"Who were they?"

Jah's eyes widened as if it finally dawned on her "Demons, I think...there was one over the other one. Though they both took pleasure in torturing me, I was standing on a hot spot of some kind, and they would point or toss something at my feet, and flames would scorch them. I don't know..." she shook her head again, "The leader would also torture the other one? This isn't making any logical sense!"

"Keep going, just get it all out; we'll sort through it after." Keziah looked her friend in the eyes to encourage her.

"Okay." Jah took a deep breath, reassuring herself that getting it out would be better than trying to sort it out from within, "They ignored me, well never acknowledged me, other than the pain they inflicted on me. They knew I was there; the more agony I was in, the more evil satisfaction was shown on the leader's face...nor did they answer me." Her voice was certain, "But I have a feeling they could hear me. I was utterly helpless. Then I began to listen," she acted out her recollections, "they said something about Job and were talking about all that had happened. The lesser one was over me. He said that I was the last straw; what could that mean? He had talked me into flinging myself out the window, but the Son of Man stopped me. I don't know what he meant or who he was talking about."

In Keziah's mind, she saw Jah fretting about the room. A sinister shaded character was coaxing her nerves as she became more and more upset. A Holy figure was sitting in the windowpane. Jah flang herself toward the window, but since the Holy One was sitting in the way, she did not go out the window but bounced off Him. The window broke from Him, slinging the demonic agitator out, and Jah hit her head on the floor.

Keziah shook her head to rejoin Jah.

"Then, I felt even worse. I let everyone down; I had messed everything up. I didn't know what to do. I was in such despair. After some time had passed, I'm not sure how much, a figure approached me and said that he knew the way out. I pressed him, and he fled, so I pursued him, but he would not wait. We reached a sunny place outside, and then he was gone. There were fresh air and a gentle breeze. I heard a voice like the voice of God. 'Just believe in Me, and you shall be saved.' Then the earth opened beneath me, and I was back in the pit from which I had come. The leader spoke to my keeper, 'She thinks she can escape!'" Jah made her voice sinister, mimicking what she had heard, "'You haven't taught her there is no escape?' Then he tortured us both."

For Keziah, this correlated with the curtains falling.

"Then I spoke to God in my heart like Job had taught me, but had never done myself before."

"What do you mean you 'had never done this before?' You taught me how to pray!"

"I just told you what Job had told me — I had never tried it myself. I never really believed in all that stuff," her face scrunched into skepticism.

Keziah didn't know what to think about that. Jah put her hand on her friend's shoulder as she stood to be wrapped in a long thin linen. Keziah helped Jah move around so that her back was to the water. The older woman sat on a sturdy stool with a back and used it for a hold as she leaned over the water. In another chair on the other side of the tub, Keziah placed her feet into the tub. She wetted and lathered Jah's long graying hair. "But being faced with utter despair," Jah looked upward as she remembered, "and to be forever tortured…I was willing to try," she admitted shaking her head, "I would have tried anything to make it stop."

"So, what happened?" Keziah was all caught up in the story. She was lathering Jah's hair for the third time now; she was trying to be mindful of the gash on her head but careful to wash all the dried blood from her matted hair.

"I said in my heart," Keziah paused as Jah looked straight into her big blue eyes upside down as she spoke, "'I don't know if You can hear me from here, but if You can, I know You are real. I believe.' That's when the cavern ceiling was ripped open." Jah reached out in front of her toward the ceiling, hands together, then once extended, she parted them like someone might be parting curtains. "The lesser demon writhed in pain from the light." She rested her hands back on her tummy as Keziah poured the pitcher of water over her hair. "This was worse for him than the torture the leader inflicted. The leader demon was yelling, 'She is mine, Son of Man, she is mine! The Father and I had a deal. All was in my control up to his life. She is mine!' That's when I looked into the light and saw arms outstretched for me." Jah stood and faced Keziah, who had just wrapped her wet head in a towel, to demonstrate. "Like a father beckoning his child into his arms," Jah flexed her fingertips in a welcoming manner. Keziah was powerless to resist, she stood, and the women embraced, weeping.

Keziah had Jah dressed and was laying her back down into her bed.

"That's when I woke to you standing over me."

Tears were streaming down both their faces. "You know that was real. Not our realm but real nonetheless."

"I feel that way, but logically it doesn't make any sense."

"I guess some things must be just too mighty for us to understand, but God saved you from that torturous place."

With a big grin of relief, Jah confirmed, "I know, I believe."

The two friends hugged again.

A knock at the door broke them apart. Jah answered it, "Come in."

Keren poked her head in, "We wanted to give you an update, but if you need your rest, we can come back later."

They could hear shuffling behind the door and beyond the girl. "No, please all come in."

Keren pushed the door all the way open and rushed around the bed and was going to sit at Jah's feet, but Keziah followed her around and ushered her closer to the middle. Keziah took the foot position, and Kadri the same on the other side; they held hands.

Jah clasped Keren's hand, which welcomed Keren to her heart. The other three gathered upon Job's bed. All were sitting on the side of the bed facing Jah.

Kadri told everything that had happened from the time he left this room last until now. The others interjected their tidbits from time to time.

When all had been told, Keziah ushered everyone out of the room. "You need your rest. I'll come to get you when dinner is ready." With the big breakfast that they had shared, neither of them noticed they had missed lunch.

"Thank you. Have Kadri try to find Job. He'll be hungry when God is through with him."

"Will do."

CHAPTER 11

After God was done with Job, he entered the main house. Everyone sprung into excited action catering to his every whim.

"We wrote most of it down word for word." Kadri was telling Job while Cale heated water for his bath, while Keren fetched him clean clothes.

"You mean the debate?" gesturing toward the barn.

"Yes, Master, God had provided for your request before you had made it."

"After dinner tonight, I want to see it."

"Of course, Job, anything you wish."

"I wish we had more than chickens to offer as a thanksgiving to God. But for now, I will settle for clean clothes. Then I want to see my wife."

"Good, because we are out of chickens, my lord."

Keren told the women upstairs, handed off Job's clothes to one of the menfolk, and rejoined the ladies. Keziah made sure Jah was dressed and ready to be reunited with her husband. Then they, with Keren, joined the men outside in the stables area.

Before going into the barn, the men approached Job, "Master, may we speak with you?"

Job stepped to the stables with them. Gilad offered his she-goat after Cale milked her one last time, and Eitan had caught three wild doves in traps he had set.

"Like I said, God provides for you before you ask. Your house is restored." Kadri offered Job a flaming torch; the woodpile was rebuilt upon Job's ash heap.

"Very good, my workers. Oh wait, you are not any longer; I released you."

"We and all of our descendants will forever be of The house of Job if you will have us." Kadri expressed the most deep-felt sentiments of all present.

"And you are all my beloved friends. More than that…family."

"Here, here!" Jah raised her glass from her seat at the large picnic table set up.

Job's heart skipped a beat. His wife was here and not in opposition to him. Job was choked up. Jah had tears in her eyes as she joined the love of her life. He hugged her close to him with his free arm.

They walked together out to the fire pit. Raising the torch high, Job said, "God of all creation, the One mightier than we, we offer You this night all that we have. We thank you for one another." Jah gave Job's waist a squeeze to indicate that she felt the same, especially about him. He looked into her eyes as he said, "For all we have, and all we do not, come from You alone." She looked intently into his eyes without blinking to show she wholeheartedly agreed with what he said to their God. "To the Ruler and Controller of everything, glory and honor to You everlastingly." Job tossed the torch on the woodpile.

In unison, everyone said, "Amen."

The flames rose high.

That night they ate outside, under the stars, at what everyone affectionately called "Keren's table," though another table was needed to accommodate them all. Job and Jah sat on one end, with Kadri and Keziah opposite them. Cale and Keren were seated to Job's right and the other two, Gilad and Eitan, to his left.

The feast was one of the grandest any of them had ever seen. After it, the ladies cleaned up, and the men retired to the main house dining area where they showed Job what they had done. Job was impressed.

"I'll add what God told me."

"I've paraphrased the first round." Cale pointed out.

"Even Keren wrote what Elihu, the youngling, spoke."

"Yes, he is the one who told me I would find God on the other side of the storm."

Jah was passing through to retire. "That statement could be taken literally or figuratively." The other two ladies were behind her.

"So true," Keziah agreed.

All the men pondered this, and all began shaking their heads in agreement.

"Will you take me to bed, my husband?" Jah whispered to Job in his ear.

"I have one question, then we will retire, all of us." All eyes were on Job.

"What's with all the beds?" He looked about.

Everyone laughed. Keren spoke, "We are literally of the house of Job." Again, laughter erupted.

Kadri offered, "We just all wanted to be close. The girls mainly."

He sniffed as if this gesture would make him seem more manly somehow, which was met with another round of laughter.

One by one, they each retired to where they had been sleeping. Except for Cale and Job: Job went to his bed, and Cale was booted outside with the other men.

CHAPTER 12

The next day, Job's face began to look normal. There were scabs where the oozing blisters once were.

By mid-morning, his friends had returned, led by Eliphaz. They brought with them a very large entourage. Each of the landlords brought seven bulls and seven rams.

Job met them just beyond the ash heap with Kadri in tow. The fire from the previous night still smoldered. Job waited for them to approach.

Eliphaz started, "On our way home yesterday, God told me He was angry with us. That we need you to pray for us if we are to escape His wrath."

Job looked at his friend squarely, "I will pray for you." Eliphaz's steward clapped his hands with a smack, jumped into action, herding everything into position.

Kadri whispered to Job, "Ask him to tell you word for word what God told him."

Job nodded, "Go get the others."

Kadri went to do Job's bidding. Job directed everyone as to proper protocol. Seven more woodpiles were added, each circling the stables that had been dismantled to accommodate all the sacrifices. Everyone from the house of Job stood near a pile with a torch in hand. The torches were lit from the original pile that Job was now standing near. Once all were in position, Kadri handed Job one of the torches. He could see his wife to the pile to his right. Next to her was Cale, then Keren next to him. Gilad, then Eitan. Between Eitan and Kadri was Keziah, with Kadri to Job's left. Job looked at each one to make sure they were all ready.

Then he began, "God of heaven and earth, Creator of all, Controller of all. I ask for Your forgiveness on behalf of Eliphaz the Temanite, Bildad the Shuhite, and Zophar the Naamathite. Do not hold against them or their households, their transgressions against You. They, too, spoke without knowledge about You as I did to You. As You have forgiven me, so also forgive them. Do not now or ever in the future withhold any blessings from them for these transgressions which You have forgiven us this day." Job tossed his torch upon his original fire.

In unison, the others followed suit, and everybody spoke together, "Amen."

Then as they began to cook the offerings, more people came from over the hill. Everyone, whom the workers had informed, was coming to comfort Job in his distress: all his brothers and sisters and other kinfolk. Job was handed a piece of money from everybody who was not from his house, along with a gold ring.

During the festivities, Gilad came and sat with Cale and Keren on a blanket at Keren's table, minus the table. "Let me get this straight. You're not Jacey's daughter?"

"No, she was my aunt."

"That means Sabah is your mother…"

"Yes."

"But she died giving birth to our baby."

"I didn't die. Wait! Are you saying you're my father?"

"I must be…We were married. Sabah was pregnant with you when I left to find work." He talked through it. "I came back too late to ever see her again…" Emotions he had held back for so long threatened to surface, "I was told you both died."

"Grandma said she was worried you would take me from them. So I was told to say Jacey was my mother if anyone I didn't know asked. When my grandparents died a few years ago, Aunt Jacey took me with her; she told people I was hers, but I think it was more to get sympathy than for any good of mine."

"I don't understand what happened to Jacey; she was a great kid from what I remember."

"I don't know. To me, she has always been wild Aunt Jacey," the girl shrugged her shoulders.

"You look a lot like your mother." Gilad looked at her discerningly and for the first time at any length.

"She has your eyes." Cale offered.

Keren blushed under all the attention. "Would either of you like more?" she rose.

Gilad hadn't touched his plate. Cale's was empty, and Keren's was half full. Gilad just shook his head.

"Sure, but I'll get it." Cale stood and got close to Keren. "You okay?" she looked unsure into his eyes but nodded that she was. "Talk to him. Get to know him. He's a great person."

She had a tear-filled eye that just would not spill. She nodded and sat back down.

Cale left them. Eitan looked as if he was going to head toward them, and Cale stopped him, "Hey, Eitan! Join me, will you?"

"I thought we were going to sit at Keren's table. I was coming to join you there."

"Gilad and Keren are talking. They need some privacy, so I moved over here."

They didn't say anything else to one another. Cale was too busy staring at them to be much company to anyone else.

Some time later, Keren got up; it was obvious that she was crying. Cale followed her to her tent.

Eitan was fuming; he joined Gilad. "What is with you, man? She's young enough to be your daughter. And anyone with eyes can see she and Cale are in love. How are you going to just butt in like that?"

"Eitan, she *is* my daughter," Gilad explained everything to him and asked what he should do. "She and I don't know each other. Do I tell Job and the others, or do we keep this to ourselves?"

Cale said nothing; he just stood behind her and rubbed her upper arms. Keren took a step back, her arms folded over her chest. He wrapped his arms over hers. "He doesn't want to tell Job, or he doesn't know if we should anyway. I asked if he was ashamed of me but didn't give him a chance to really answer. He was shocked by my question, I think."

"I was about five when he came back from learning your mom had passed, but I remember he was devastated. When I began being trained to be a shepherd, he was my instructor. We spent many days together back then. Though he didn't like talking about it, he told me he loved your mother like Jah and Job, or my parents do each other. He was really looking forward to being a dad. He thought and had accepted he never would be. Give him some time to digest the fact that God has given him his heart's desire." She turned to face Cale and was crying. He held her. The flap behind him opened. He glanced to see Gilad looking sheepishly.

Keren wouldn't let go of Cale when he tried to step back. She just stared at Gilad.

"I'm not, nor have I ever been, nor do I think I will ever be ashamed of you. I want to tell Job. I want to tell the world. I want to scream it from the mountain tops, 'My daughter lives!' and that you are she." Gilad stretched his arm out toward her. She let go of Cale and rushed to Gilad. Eitan, standing outside, blew his nose into a handkerchief. "We could go now and tell Job and the others, or we can wait to tell them after the festivities are over and when it is just us. The choice is yours."

"I, too, want to tell the world 'I have a dad' and 'he loves me' and that you are he, but I think it will be best if we wait to tell the others. When it is just us."

He jerked his head in agreement. Then, without letting her go, he twisted back to look at Eitan and then again forward to address Cale. "Are we all in agreement? We will inform the others, once all who are not of the house of Job are gone?"

Pressed against his chest, Keren shook her head in the affirmative while the other two simply replied, "Yes."

Cale spoke up. "Okay, so does this mean we can all rejoin the party? I could go for another plate." Everyone laughed.

"Me too!" Keren said through a tear-stricken smile.

"I'll go get us both one. You may want to wash your face, so no one knows you've been crying." Gilad stroked her lovely face. His eyes turned bloodshot as a tear formed.

"Oh, Daddy." she kissed his cheek, then went to the water basin and fetched a couple of rags. Eitan entered the humble home. When Keren returned, she had to go back for two more for Cale and Eitan. She chuckled at them all. "Grandpa always said I had a way of making grown men cry. And I thought he was talking only about himself," she laughed again, and the men joined her. They left her house and joined the party.

CHAPTER 13

Job's house was truly restored. Just as everyone was leaving, Job showed his friends the project of the record of the debate and promised to let them know once it was finished. They were impressed and in agreement with the accuracy of the account.

Gilad and Keren, with Cale and Eitan in tow, announced to Job and the others the news of them being blood kin. Cale worked unnoticed at getting the ladies busy in the kitchen and all the men to themselves. "I've got one question...Whom do I ask for permission for Keren to be my bride?"

Job, who was standing beside Gilad, chapped his hand upon his friend's back, "I'm not so sure this man is worthy of such a lovely woman as your daughter," he winked.

Gilad, with a twinkle in his eye, announced, "No but any man would be a blessed man to have him as a son-in-law."

Job handed the boy one of the smaller rings that had been handed to him the night before.

Cale was shocked. His dad clipped him on the shoulder, "No time like the present, Son."

Job called for the ladies. His and Kadri's wives stood behind them respectively. Kadri sat to his left and Gilad to his right. Across from him, Cale and Keren were seated next to their respective fathers. So that Eitan wasn't left out, he stood hind, yet between the couple. Terms were laid out, and the two were betrothed together for the next year to prepare for their union, of which Job would officiate.

During that time, Jah had their first new addition to the House of Job. It was a girl; Job named her after the most wonderful woman he could think of — his wife.

After the wedding, Job's friends gave him fabric for binding the debate. The women embroidered the words onto the material. The goatskin from Eitan's ewe was used for its cover.

Jah insisted that nothing of her story be added to the record. However, after more probing into her 'dream,' Keziah added what she believed in her heart had happened in the ethereal realm. All were in agreement with this.

The register was not finished until Keren-happuch was born. The last of Job and Jah's ten blessings after God had taken the first ten. In order by birth, the litter was thus: Jah short for Jemimah (the first daughter named after her mother), Elkin (the first son), Anat (the second son), Bartek (the third son), Keziah (the second daughter, named after the second greatest woman Job knew), Hillel (the fourth son), Toma & Tomek (the fifth & sixth sons, twins), Gilon (the seventh son), and Keren-happuch (the third daughter, named after the greatest young lady Job knew). The girls were the most fair of any and were given an inheritance along with their brothers.

Keziah and Kadri, as well as Keren and Cale, all added to the number of them, though none exceeded Job and Jah. Their sons and daughters wedded one to another.

They all lived close to the main house of Job, and every night the extensive House of Job would gather for the sacrifices of thanksgiving and praise to the Controller of all — God.

By the end of Job's life, God had blessed the House of Job twice as much in every way from when He allowed his possessions and blessings to be stripped from him.

Jah's life ended happily; she with Job had the blessings of seeing out to the fourth generations from the original House of Job, who had survived that tragic day.

The scar on her heart never faded. Job erected a memorial to those who passed from this life that day at the site where Erel's house had stood, and it housed The book: Of the House of Job.

The day they dedicated the spot was one of only three times Jah had made the trip. The first one, the site was bare, and Erel had brought her and his dad out to pitch the idea to them, then the day the house was completed, and that somber day.

Jah, Keren, and Keziah, along with the smallest of the children, rode out in a large wagon with Eitan driving. Job, Kadri, Cale, and Gilad each had one or two of the older children on their mounts with them, and the oldest of the children were riding unattended. There was a reading of the book and a moment of dedication. Then all returned back to the main homestead.

On the way back, most of the children were napping in the wagon. Jah began to reflect, "You know I didn't really believe in Job's God until all of this."

Keziah replied, "That still baffles me…I believed because of how strongly you and Job and Kadri believed when I first came to the house of Job."

"Either I was really good at faking it, or Kadri and Job's belief overshadowed my disbelief…"

Keren timidly asked, "How do you know if you really believe?"

Keziah, in her matter of fact manner, disclosed, "You just believe."

Gilad, who had been riding close by the wagon, chimed in, "But it isn't just knowing with your head. It is deeper, like knowing in your heart."

By this time, they were entering the barn to unhook all the mounts and turn them out. The men tended to the animals while the women were letting the children finish their naps in the wagon.

Job came close to Jah and put his loving hand on her shoulder, "I had no idea you did not fully believe until the day you met me out here." Job had no intention of bringing any shame on his wife. Nonetheless, guilt covered her face, and all there knew exactly what day he was referring to.

"That was the beginning of it all," Jah sheepishly admitted.

Cale, to redirect the conversation off of Jah, interrupted, "I know I am fairly young, but I didn't really believe myself until recently."

"Oh?" his parents answered in unison.

"Like Jah, I'm guessing, I was just going along with what I had been taught and what everyone seemed to expect of me. It wasn't until I was out all alone tending sheep that Job's God became real to me."

"Exactly!" Jah agreed, "At first, I believed because Job believed, but now I believe because I believe."

Eitan retorted, "I had a similar experience; I was isolated away from all others, just some of the animals. It was a stormy night. I was scared and alone. But in the midst of it, I chose to trust that Job's God was not going to let anything happen to Job's property…and I was included."

In remembrance, Job recalled, "That was the winter just before Gilad joined us."

"Yep, and it was just a timely thing when Gilad came on board. My faith was fresh, and I was able to guide Gilad through it all," Eitah added.

Gilad, "Yeah, I was so bitter when I first got here. I was grateful to have a place to live, but this wasn't what or how I thought my life was supposed to go," He looked affectionately towards his daughter Keren.

Kadri grabbed an old stool used for milking and placed it soundly beneath him. "It's like me grabbing this stool. I trust it is going to hold me." He jumped up and offered to help his daughter-in-law down from the wagon and offered the stool as a step, "Now it's your turn…do you trust this stool to hold you?"

Keren finagled herself out of the wagon and onto the stool with both feet planted, let go of Kadri, and, with both hands raised high, shouted, "I believe! I believe!"

The End

CPSIA information can be obtained
at www.ICGtesting.com
Printed in the USA
BVHW041101150521
607436BV00003B/715

9 781647 739430